NATIONAL GEOGRAPHIC
THEME SETS™

MW01689392

Using Earth's Resources

TEACHER'S GUIDE • SCIENCE

NATIONAL GEOGRAPHIC
School Publishing

PICTURE CREDIT
page 64 © ART on FILE/CORBIS

Produced through the worldwide resources of the National Geographic Society, John M. Fahey, Jr., President and Chief Executive Officer; Gilbert M. Grosvenor, Chairman of the Board; Nina D. Hoffman, Executive Vice President and President, Books and Education Publishing Group.

PREPARED BY NATIONAL GEOGRAPHIC SCHOOL PUBLISHING
Ericka Markman, Senior Vice President and President, Children's Books and Education Publishing Group; Steve Mico, Senior Vice President and Editorial Director; Marianne Hiland, Executive Editor; Richard Easby, Editorial Manager; Jim Hiscott, Design Manager; Kristin Hanneman, Illustrations Manager; Matt Wascavage, Manager of Publishing Services; Sean Philpotts, Production Manager; Jane Ponton, Production Artist.

MANUFACTURING AND QUALITY MANAGEMENT
Christopher A. Liedel, Chief Financial Officer; Phillip L. Schlosser, Director; Clifton M. Brown III, Manager.

PROGRAM CONSULTANTS
Dr. Shirley V. Dickson, Ph.D. Educational Consultant; Margit E. McGuire, Ph.D., Professor of Teacher Education and Social Studies, Seattle University; James A. Shymansky, E Desmond Lee Professor of Science Education, University of Missouri-St Louis.

PROGRAM REVIEWERS
Sylvia Roe Bath, Teacher, Lake Zurich, Illinois CUSD 95; Randee Blair, Curriculum Coordinator, Evanston/Skokie, Illinois School District 65; Patty Frank, Teacher, Creighton, Arizona School District; Bonnie Goodrich, Learning Specialist, Plymouth-Canton, Michigan Community School District; Mary Ann Groke, Teacher, Jefferson County, Colorado Public Schools; Ann Hopkins, Literacy Strategy Coach, Fairfield-Suisun, California Unified School District; Joanne C. Letwinch, Teacher, Haddonfield, New Jersey Public Schools; Lynn Levin, Reading Specialist, Fairfax County, Virginia Public Schools; Kirk Robbins, Teacher, Renton, Washington School District; Stephani Wise, Teacher, Richardson, Texas Independent School District.

TEACHER'S GUIDE DEVELOPMENT
Morrison BookWorks, LLC

Published by the National Geographic Society
1145 17th Street, N.W.
Washington, D.C. 20036-4688

ISBN: 0-7922-4923-2

Product Number 4P 42123

First Printing January, 2005

Contents

Program Overview

- About the Program 4
- Program Components 6
- Developing Literacy Skills 10
- Flexible Use 11
- Pacing Guide 12
- Differentiated Instruction 14
- Research-Based Instruction 16
- Factors Affecting Readability 18
- Placing Students in Levels 20
- Supporting English Language Learners 22
- Assessing Progress 26
- Extend Your Reading 28

Theme Overview 30

Lesson 1 34

Lesson 2 39

Lesson 3 43

Lesson 4 47

Lesson 5 51

Extend the Learning 55

Activity and Assessment Masters 58

Activity Masters 59

Assessment Tests 73

- Open-Book Test 73
- Tests 74

Test Answers 82

About the Program

"Making A Difference Means Making It Different."

From Position Statement of the International Reading Association (March 2000)

One size does not fit all

Today's students come from a variety of cultural and language backgrounds, socioeconomic levels, and academic levels. Educators realize one size does not fit all, so no one book can meet the needs of all students.

The **Theme Sets** program provides differentiated resources for teachers to meet the diverse needs of their students. Each ***Theme Set*** provides four books crafted to match the wide range of reading levels within each classroom. All books provide the same core concepts but within different contexts and at different reading levels. For students who struggle with content-area textbooks, the **Theme Sets** provide core curriculum that is broken down, not watered down. For students who are reading on grade level, the **Theme Sets** provide literacy and core content curriculum with appropriate challenge and support. For students who need more challenging material, the **Theme Sets** provide literacy and core content in ways that develop students' critical thinking skills.

Equity in education is every child's right

Equity in education is tied to students' access to quality curriculum, materials, and teaching. Yet students, especially those who struggle with reading, are often denied access to core content. It is essential that these students have access to grade-level curriculum to prevent the knowledge gap from widening as they proceed through the grades. The **Theme Sets** offer grade-level curriculum to students across a wide range of reading levels. The **Theme Sets** also support students as they develop reading and writing strategies and skills.

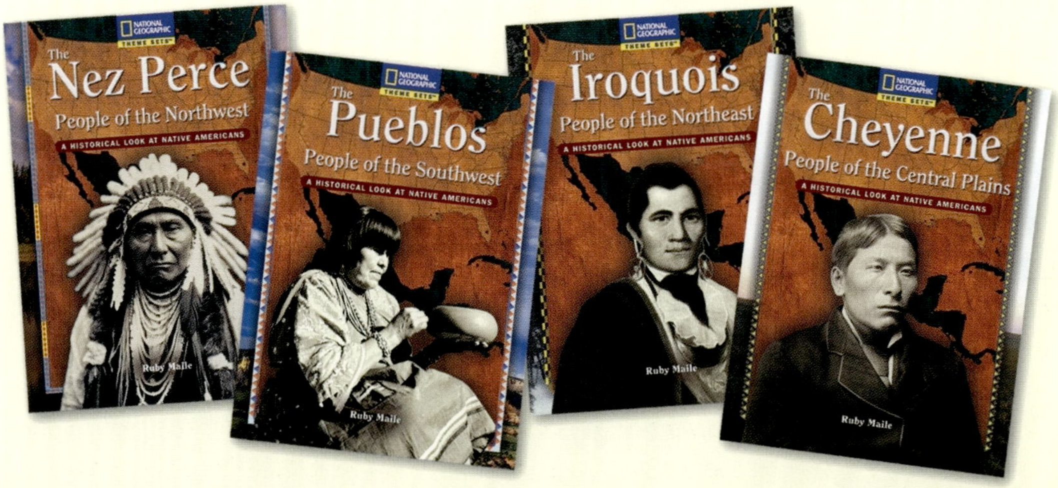

Program Goals

National Geographic School Publishing is committed to providing the highest quality materials that meet the diverse needs of teachers and students.

The Theme Sets offer materials that

- **facilitate differentiated instruction.**
- **promote educational equity through access for all students.**
- **provide essential standards-based curriculum in science and social studies.**
- **support the developmental needs of students at a variety of reading levels.**
- **provide explicit instruction in vocabulary and comprehension strategies.**
- **develop fluency.**
- **offer comprehensive teaching materials that streamline teacher planning.**

Program Consultants

Shirley Dickson, Ph.D. is an educational consultant in literacy for kindergarten through the secondary grades. She consults on reading research projects and works with states as they develop and implement state literacy policy. Dr. Dickson's current work includes research in preventing reading difficulties in kindergarten through grade 3. Her expertise is the design of effective and comprehensive reading instruction for typical and struggling learners. Dr. Dickson is a former Director of Literacy for the Education Commission of the States; Director of Statewide Curriculum Initiatives for Texas, including the Reading and Math Initiatives; Director of Reading for Texas; professor in literacy and special education at Northern Illinois University; and special educator.

Margit E. McGuire, Ph.D. is Director and Professor of Teacher Education at Seattle University and a former president of the National Council for the Social Studies. She is the recipient of the Washington Award for Excellence in Teacher Preparation and has presented nationally and internationally on topics related to social studies and teacher preparation. She is the author of the Storypath Program and is engaged in a number of research projects on the Storypath approach both in Seattle, Washington, and Sydney, Australia.

James A. Shymansky, Ph.D. is an E. Desmond Lee Professor of Science Education at the University of Missouri-St. Louis. He currently directs the "Science Cooperatives Project," a five-year NSF systemic reform effort involving 1,200 elementary school teachers from 36 school districts in rural Missouri and Iowa. He has authored an elementary science textbook series and a K–12 science review series. He has also authored more than a hundred research publications, book chapters, and monographs on teaching and learning elementary school science. He is the past editor of the *Journal of Research in Science Teaching* and currently senior editor of the *International Journal of Science and Mathematics Education* and President-Elect of the National Association for Research in Science Teaching.

Program Components

Student Books

Each ***Theme Set*** includes four books on different topics. Each book is written at a different reading level and focuses on a specific topic to explain and illustrate the central theme.

All four books are firmly connected together. They all develop a common set of Key Concepts and core vocabulary. The goal is that all students acquire essential core content at their own reading levels.

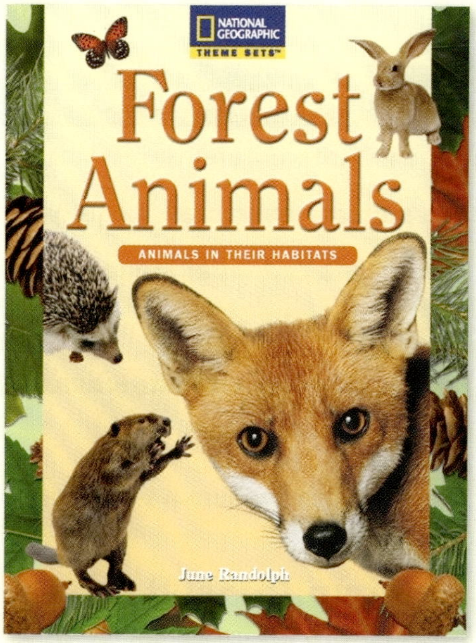

Level A

Social Studies Themes	Book Titles			
	Level A	Level B	Level C	Level D
A Historical Look at Native Americans	The Nez Perce: People of the Northwest	The Pueblos: People of the Southwest	The Iroquois: People of the Northeast	Cheyenne: People of the Central Plains
Communication Around the World	Telephone	Radio	Television	Internet
Communities and Their Locations	Missoula, Montana	Boston, Massachusetts	St. Louis, Missouri	Honolulu, Hawaii
Cultures and Celebrations	Mexico	Italy	Japan	Egypt
Immigration to the United States	Irish Immigration	Chinese Immigration	Mexican Immigration	German-Jewish Immigration
Inventions Bring Change	The Reaper	The Railroad	Water-Powered Mills	The Cotton Gin
Providing Goods	From Cotton to Blue Jeans	From Trees to Paper	From Wheat to Bread	From Cows to Ice Cream
Trade Across Time and Cultures	Silk	Spices	Salt	Fur

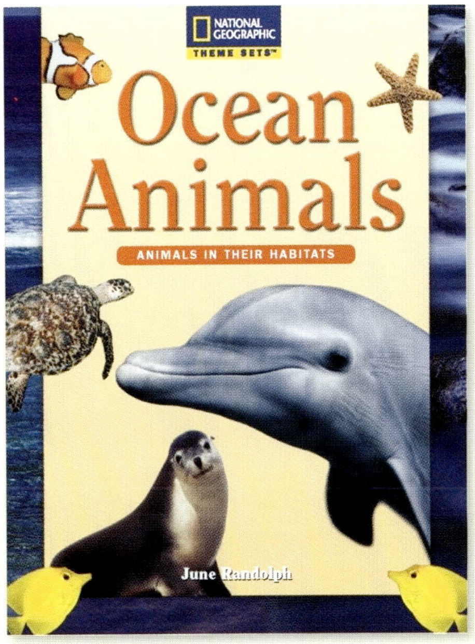

Level B

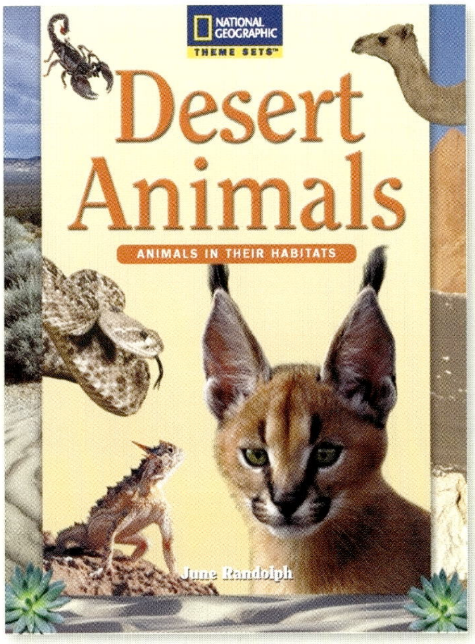

Level C

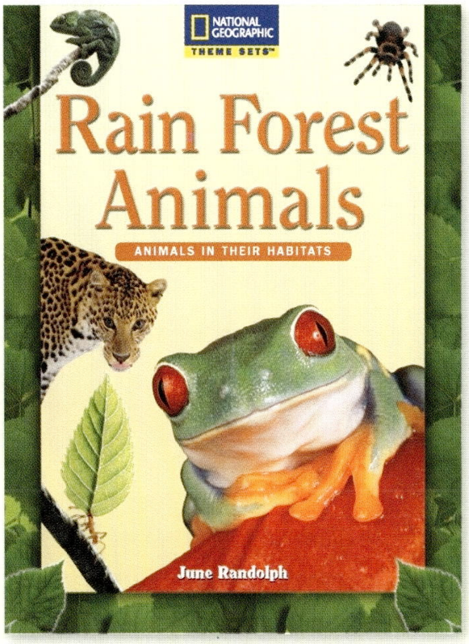

Level D

Science Themes	Book Titles			
	Level A	Level B	Level C	Level D
Animals in Their Habitats	Forest Animals	Ocean Animals	Desert Animals	Rain Forest Animals
Cells at Work	Skin	Muscles	Blood	Bone
Energy	Energy in the Home	Energy in the Factory	Energy at the Airport	Energy at the Sports Arena
Extreme Weather	Droughts	Floods	Tornadoes	Hurricanes
Life Cycles	Giant Pandas	Monarch Butterflies	Poison Dart Frogs	Komodo Dragons
Shaping Earth's Surface	Wind	Water	Ice	Earthquakes and Volcanoes
Using Earth's Resources	Indonesia's Rain Forests	Greenland's Ocean Region	Australia's Deserts	Peru's Mountains
Using Simple Machines	Machines in the Home	Machines in Sports	Machines in Construction	Machines in Health

Student Book Features

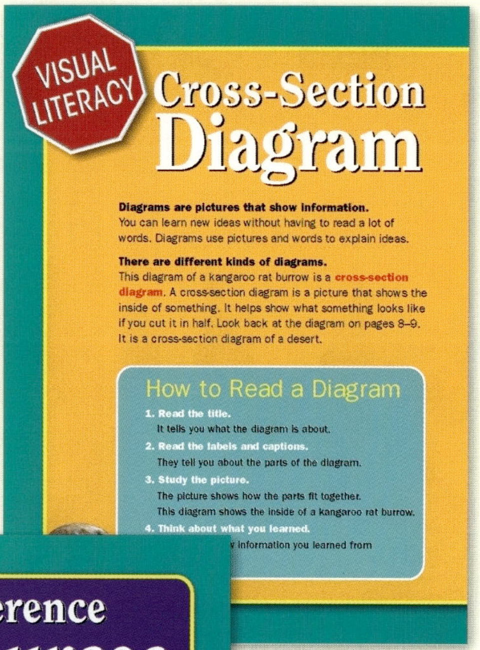
VISUAL LITERACY

Cross-Section Diagram

Diagrams are pictures that show information.
You can learn new ideas without having to read a lot of words. Diagrams use pictures and words to explain ideas.

There are different kinds of diagrams.
This diagram of a kangaroo rat burrow is a **cross-section diagram**. A cross-section diagram is a picture that shows the inside of something. It helps show what something looks like if you cut it in half. Look back at the diagram on pages 8–9. It is a cross-section diagram of a desert.

How to Read a Diagram

1. **Read the title.**
   It tells you what the diagram is about.
2. **Read the labels and captions.**
   They tell you about the parts of the diagram.
3. **Study the picture.**
   The picture shows how the parts fit together.
   This diagram shows the inside of a kangaroo rat burrow.
4. **Think about what you learned.**
   … information you learned from

Visual Literacy

Each ***Theme Set*** includes explicit instruction in one visual literacy skill. Students are shown how to read and use diagrams, maps, graphs, and other examples of visual information.

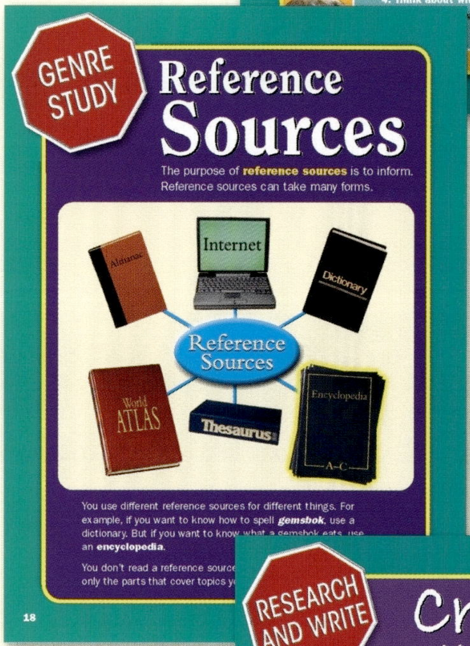
GENRE STUDY

Reference Sources

The purpose of **reference sources** is to inform. Reference sources can take many forms.

You use different reference sources for different things. For example, if you want to know how to spell ***gemsbok***, use a dictionary. But if you want to know what a gemsbok eats, use an **encyclopedia**.

You don't read a reference source … only the parts that cover topics y…

18

Genre Study

Each ***Theme Set*** focuses on one nonfiction writing genre form. The genre is defined and explained to students. At the same time, students see how the genre is connected to the subject matter of the ***Theme Set***. Genres covered in the **Theme Sets** program include, biographies, how-to books, compare and contrast article, news report, reference sources, and others.

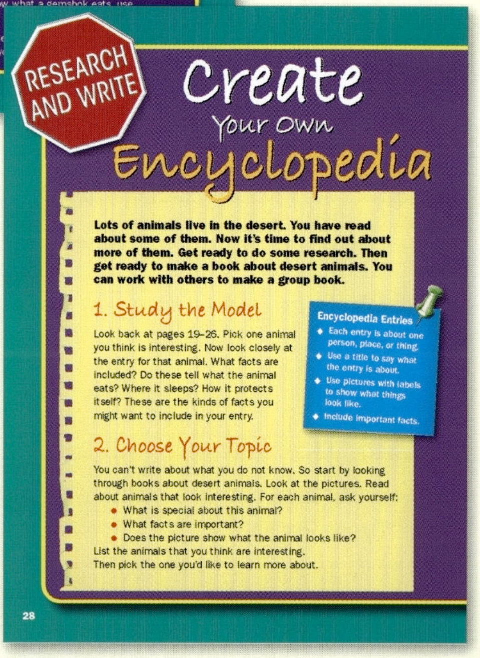
RESEARCH AND WRITE

Create Your Own Encyclopedia

Lots of animals live in the desert. You have read about some of them. Now it's time to find out about more of them. Get ready to do some research. Then get ready to make a book about desert animals. You can work with others to make a group book.

1. Study the Model

Look back at pages 19–26. Pick one animal you think is interesting. Now look closely at the entry for that animal. What facts are included? Do these tell what the animal eats? Where it sleeps? How it protects itself? These are the kinds of facts you might want to include in your entry.

Encyclopedia Entries
- Each entry is about one person, place, or thing.
- Use a title to say what the entry is about.
- Use pictures with labels to show what things look like.
- Include important facts.

2. Choose Your Topic

You can't write about what you do not know. So start by looking through books about desert animals. Look at the pictures. Read about animals that look interesting. For each animal, ask yourself:
- What is special about this animal?
- What facts are important?
- Does the picture show what the animal looks like?

List the animals that you think are interesting.
Then pick the one you'd like to learn more about.

28

Research and Write

Students have the opportunity to practice their own researching and writing skills by creating their own work based on the genre study they have learned about in the books.

Teacher's Guide Features

Each ***Theme Set*** has a separate Teacher's Guide that provides clear instructional guidelines and comprehensive instructional plans.

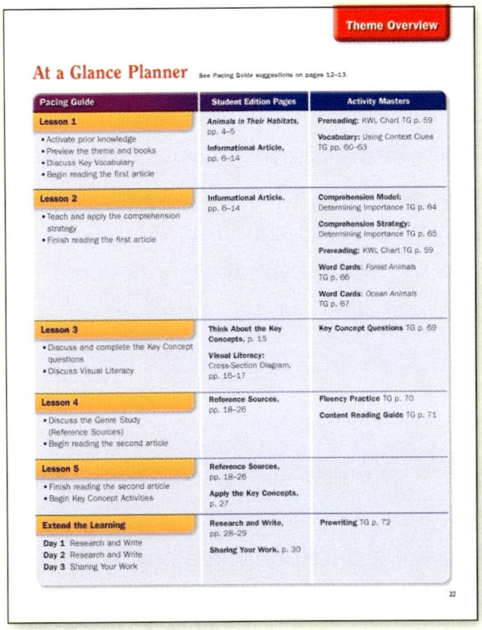

Theme Overview

At a Glance Planner See Pacing Guide suggestions on pages 12–13.

Pacing Guide	Student Edition Pages	Activity Masters
Lesson 1 • Activate prior knowledge • Preview the theme and books • Discuss Key Vocabulary • Begin reading the first article	***Animals in Their Habitats,*** pp. 4–5 **Informational Article,** pp. 6–14	**Prereading:** KWL Chart TG p. 59 **Vocabulary:** Using Context Clues TG pp. 60–63
Lesson 2 • Teach and apply the comprehension strategy • Finish reading the first article	**Informational Article,** pp. 6–14	**Comprehension Model:** Determining Importance TG p. 64 **Comprehension Strategy:** Determining Importance TG p. 65 **Prereading:** KWL Chart TG p. 59 **Word Cards:** *Forest Animals* TG p. 66 **Word Cards:** *Ocean Animals* TG p. 67
Lesson 3 • Discuss and complete the Key Concept questions • Discuss Visual Literacy	**Think About the Key Concepts,** p. 15 **Visual Literacy:** Cross-Section Diagram, pp. 16–17	**Key Concept Questions** TG p. 69
Lesson 4 • Discuss the Genre Study (Reference Sources) • Begin reading the second article	**Reference Sources,** pp. 18–26	**Fluency Practice** TG p. 70 **Content Reading Guide** TG p. 71
Lesson 5 • Finish reading the second article • Begin Key Concept Activities	**Reference Sources,** pp. 18–26 **Apply the Key Concepts,** p. 27	
Extend the Learning **Day 1** Research and Write **Day 2** Research and Write **Day 3** Sharing Your Work	**Research and Write,** pp. 28–29 **Sharing Your Work,** p. 30	**Prewriting** TG p. 72

33

Planning Guides

Each guide contains planning guides to help you effectively manage instructional time.

Lesson 1

Begin Reading: Pages 6–14 Small Groups

	Forest Animals	Ocean Animals	Desert Animals	Rain Forest Animals
First Activity Block	With the Teacher **Begin Reading** • Introduce words difficult for students to read. • Introduce book vocabulary. • Begin reading the article in sections. • Check comprehension following each section.	*Pairs* **Vocabulary** Using Context Clues To each student, distribute the *Ocean Vocabulary* Master. Students can work in pairs to complete this Master.	*Pairs* **Vocabulary** Using Context Clues To each student, distribute the *Desert Vocabulary* Master. Students can work in pairs to complete this Master.	*Pairs* **Vocabulary** Using Context Clues To each student, distribute the *Rain Forest Vocabulary* Master. Students can work in pairs to complete this Master.
Second Activity Block	*Pairs* **Vocabulary** Using Context Clues To each student, distribute the *Forest Vocabulary* Master. Students can work in pairs to complete this Master.	With the Teacher **Begin Reading** • Introduce words difficult for students to read. • Introduce book vocabulary. • Begin reading the article in sections. • Check comprehension following each section.	*Individuals* **Independent Reading** Students begin reading *Animals of the Desert*, Student Book pages 6–14. Students can use their *Prereading* Masters to check their ideas, add information, and write questions they may have.	*Individuals* **Independent Reading** Students begin reading *Animals of the Rain Forest*, Student Book pages 6–14. Students can use their *Prereading* Masters to check their ideas, add information, and write questions they may have.

36

Lesson Plans

Each guide contains comprehensive lesson plans that help you customize instruction.

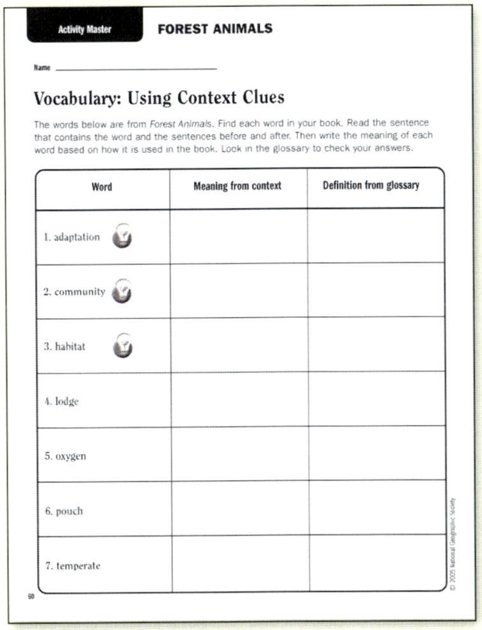

Activity Master **FOREST ANIMALS**

Name ________________

Vocabulary: Using Context Clues

The words below are from *Forest Animals*. Find each word in your book. Read the sentence that contains the word and the sentences before and after. Then write the meaning of each word based on how it is used in the book. Look in the glossary to check your answers.

Word	Meaning from context	Definition from glossary
1. adaptation		
2. community		
3. habitat		
4. lodge		
5. oxygen		
6. pouch		
7. temperate		

60

© 2005 National Geographic Society

Activity Masters

Each guide contains Activity Masters to reinforce core skills and strategies.

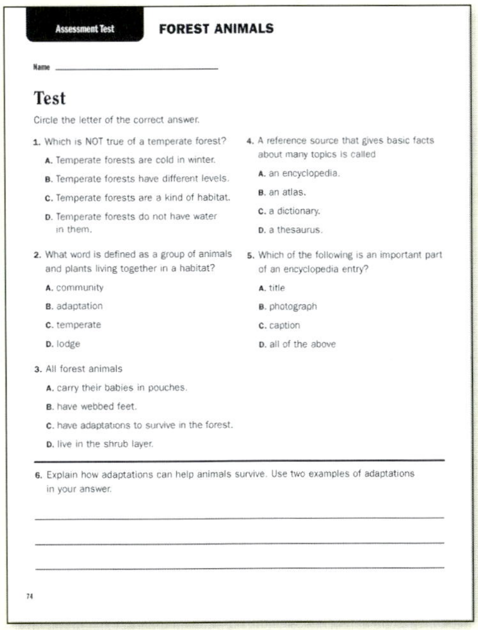

Assessment Test **FOREST ANIMALS**

Name ________________

Test

Circle the letter of the correct answer.

1. Which is NOT true of a temperate forest?
   A. Temperate forests are cold in winter.
   B. Temperate forests have different levels.
   C. Temperate forests are a kind of habitat.
   D. Temperate forests do not have water in them.
2. What word is defined as a group of animals and plants living together in a habitat?
   A. community
   B. adaptation
   C. temperate
   D. lodge
3. All forest animals
   A. carry their babies in pouches.
   B. have webbed feet.
   C. have adaptations to survive in the forest.
   D. live in the shrub layer.
4. A reference source that gives basic facts about many topics is called
   A. an encyclopedia.
   B. an atlas.
   C. a dictionary.
   D. a thesaurus.
5. Which of the following is an important part of an encyclopedia entry?
   A. title
   B. photograph
   C. caption
   D. all of the above
6. Explain how adaptations can help animals survive. Use two examples of adaptations in your answer.

____

____

____

74

Assessment

Each guide contains book-level assessments to help you measure student progress.

Developing Literacy Skills

The **Theme Sets** program supports developing readers and writers by providing appropriate scaffolding and challenges that match the needs of a wide range of students.

Vocabulary

Within each theme, essential content words are targeted as Key Vocabulary and explicitly taught to all students before reading. As students read, they encounter these words repeatedly within rich contexts and have opportunities to use the words in oral and written activities. In addition to the Key Vocabulary covered in all four books, specific book-level words are taught and used in small group and independent activities.

Comprehension

Each theme targets one specific comprehension strategy so that students learn and apply that strategy as they read. These strategies include determining importance, making connections, visualizing, asking questions, making inferences, and synthesizing. Teaching notes provide step-by-step help for explicit instruction, modeling, guided practice, and independent practice.

Visual Literacy

Understanding how to read diagrams, maps, graphs, charts, and other visual aids is critical to comprehending nonfiction. Each theme provides explicit instruction and practice in one kind of visual aid so that students learn how to extract and interpret information that is presented visually.

Text Structure and Genres

For each theme, the characteristics of one nonfiction genre/text structure are explicitly taught in the Genre Study. The second article in each Student Book serves as a model of that genre. Students also apply their understanding of that genre by writing a piece that uses that specific genre as an organizational pattern.

Research and Write

The Research and Write lesson that concludes each book in a theme provides students with an opportunity to show what they have learned. They research additional information about the topic covered in their book and then write in the specific nonfiction form that is the focus of the Genre Study and modeled in the second article.

Flexible Use

Flexibility is a critical factor in the differentiated classroom. The **THEME SETS** program is designed to provide teachers with the flexibility needed to make sure that every child succeeds and has access to core content.

Flexible to Fit a Variety of Programs

Core instruction: The **THEME SETS** are designed to be used as part of your core curriculum. They provide essential and high interest content for many of the core content areas in science and social studies. Use one or more ***Theme Sets*** instead of content-area texts.

Supplemental: The **THEME SETS** can also be used as a supplement to your content-area texts and reading program. They provide extended opportunities for students to explore core content in depth. Students will also learn more as they read the content at their own reading level.

Tutorial: The **THEME SETS** program is ideally suited to special tutorial programs such as summer school or after school programs. Educators can select those themes that fit their curriculum objectives. The **THEME SETS** program also offers versatility. Each book in a theme is divided into several parts.

Flexible Grouping

The **THEME SETS** program encourages the teacher to use flexible grouping in the classroom.

Whole Class

The teacher previews the books with the whole class and introduces the Key Concepts and Key Vocabulary.

Small Groups

The teacher can assign books based on reading ability or by the student's interest in the topic. However, groups do not necessarily have to be homogeneous. Students can also be grouped across ability levels so that they can help each other learn. The **THEME SETS** Teacher's Guide provides lessons for both homogeneous and heterogeneous grouping.

Whole Class

By bringing the whole class together again the teacher has the opportunity to check students' understanding of the big ideas of the theme. Students also have the opportunity to share their learning with others.

Pacing Guide

The **Theme Sets** program includes easy-to-follow pacing. This provides the flexibility needed to custom fit instruction to scheduling needs. The following charts show two pacing plans, one for five 90-minute lessons and one for ten 45-minute lessons.

90-minute pacing	5 Days	Teacher's Guide Pages
Lesson 1		
Day 1:	Introduce the Theme	page 34
	Introduce the Books	page 34–35
	Begin Reading: Pages 6–16 First Activity Block Second Activity Block	pages 36–37
	Check Understanding	page 38
Lesson 2		
Day 2:	Introduce Comprehension Strategy	page 39
	Finish Reading: Pages 6–16 First Activity Block Second Activity Block	pages 40–41
	Check Understanding	page 42
Lesson 3		
Day 3:	Share Learning	page 43
	Think About Key Concept Questions	page 44–45
	Visual Literacy	page 46
Lesson 4		
Day 4:	Introduce Genre Study	page 47
	Begin Reading: Pages 21–26 First Activity Block Second Activity Block	pages 48–49
	Check Understanding	page 50
Lesson 5		
Day 5:	Introduce Key Concept Activities	page 51
	Finish Reading: Pages 21–26 First Activity Block Second Activity Block	pages 52–53
	Check Understanding	page 54
Extend the Learning		
Day 1:	Research and Write	page 55
Day 2:	Research and Write	page 56
Day 3:	Sharing Your Work	page 57

45-minute pacing	10 Days	Teacher's Guide Pages
Lesson 1		
Day 1:	Introduce the Theme	page 34
	Introduce the Books	page 34–35
	Begin Reading: Pages 6–16 First Activity Block	pages 36–37
Day 2:	Begin Reading: Pages 6–16 Second Activity Block	pages 36–37
	Check Understanding	page 38
Lesson 2		
Day 3:	Introduce Comprehension Strategy	page 39
	Finish Reading: Pages 6–16 First Activity Block	pages 40–41
Day 4:	Finish Reading: Pages 6–16 Second Activity Block	pages 40–41
	Check Understanding	page 42
Lesson 3		
Day 5:	Share Learning	page 43
Day 6:	Think About Key Concept Questions	page 44–45
	Visual Literacy	page 46
Lesson 4		
Day 7:	Introduce Genre Study	page 47
	Begin Reading: Pages 21–26 First Activity Block	pages 48–49
Day 8:	Begin Reading: Pages 21–26 Second Activity Block	pages 48–49
	Check Understanding	page 50
Lesson 5		
Day 9:	Introduce Key Concept Activities	page 51
	Finish Reading: Pages 21–26 First Activity Block	pages 52–53
Day 10:	Finish Reading: Pages 21–26 Second Activity Block	pages 52–53
	Check Understanding	page 54
Extend the Learning		
Day 1:	Research and Write	page 55
Day 2:	Research and Write	page 56
Day 3:	Sharing Your Work	page 57

Differentiated Instruction

Although the concept of differentiation is simple, the implementation can be challenging. Differentiation is based on the fact that every child is unique and that classroom instruction should adapt to meet student differences. Many educators agree that instruction should have the flexibility and relevance to address the various readiness levels and learning preferences that are present in every classroom.

The **THEME SETS** program is designed to provide equal access to core content for all students at varying reading levels. The detailed lesson plan encourages flexibility in grouping students. The content provides essential core learning, and the four reading levels provide access for all. Materials are designed so teachers have the tools and information they need to implement a differentiated instructional model.

Flexible Grouping

Students will benefit from a flexible working environment where the teacher includes whole class, small group, and individual instruction that takes into account the ability and readiness of each student in the class.

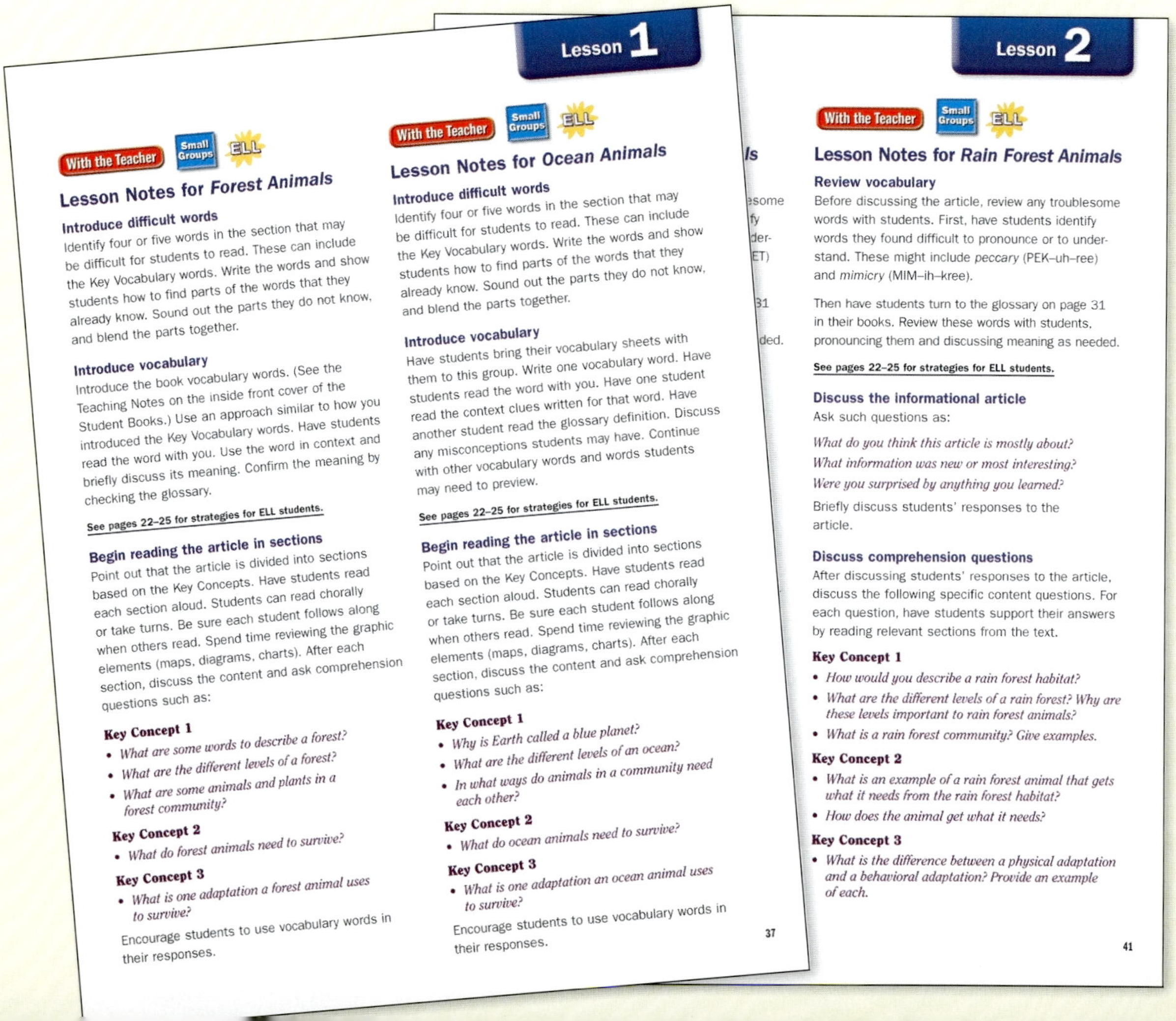

With the Teacher | Small Groups | ELL

Lesson Notes for *Forest Animals*

Introduce difficult words
Identify four or five words in the section that may be difficult for students to read. These can include the Key Vocabulary words. Write the words and show students how to find parts of the words that they already know. Sound out the parts they do not know, and blend the parts together.

Introduce vocabulary
Introduce the book vocabulary words. (See the Teaching Notes on the inside front cover of the Student Books.) Use an approach similar to how you introduced the Key Vocabulary words. Have students read the word with you. Use the word in context and briefly discuss its meaning. Confirm the meaning by checking the glossary.

See pages 22–25 for strategies for ELL students.

Begin reading the article in sections
Point out that the article is divided into sections based on the Key Concepts. Have students read each section aloud. Students can read chorally or take turns. Be sure each student follows along when others read. Spend time reviewing the graphic elements (maps, diagrams, charts). After each section, discuss the content and ask comprehension questions such as:

Key Concept 1
- *What are some words to describe a forest?*
- *What are the different levels of a forest?*
- *What are some animals and plants in a forest community?*

Key Concept 2
- *What do forest animals need to survive?*

Key Concept 3
- *What is one adaptation a forest animal uses to survive?*

Encourage students to use vocabulary words in their responses.

Lesson 1

With the Teacher | Small Groups | ELL

Lesson Notes for *Ocean Animals*

Introduce difficult words
Identify four or five words in the section that may be difficult for students to read. These can include the Key Vocabulary words. Write the words and show students how to find parts of the words that they already know. Sound out the parts they do not know, and blend the parts together.

Introduce vocabulary
Have students bring their vocabulary sheets with them to this group. Write one vocabulary word. Have students read the word with you. Have one student read the context clues written for that word. Have another student read the glossary definition. Discuss any misconceptions students may have. Continue with other vocabulary words and words students may need to preview.

See pages 22–25 for strategies for ELL students.

Begin reading the article in sections
Point out that the article is divided into sections based on the Key Concepts. Have students read each section aloud. Students can read chorally or take turns. Be sure each student follows along when others read. Spend time reviewing the graphic elements (maps, diagrams, charts). After each section, discuss the content and ask comprehension questions such as:

Key Concept 1
- *Why is Earth called a blue planet?*
- *What are the different levels of an ocean?*
- *In what ways do animals in a community need each other?*

Key Concept 2
- *What do ocean animals need to survive?*

Key Concept 3
- *What is one adaptation an ocean animal uses to survive?*

Encourage students to use vocabulary words in their responses.

37

Lesson 2

With the Teacher | Small Groups | ELL

Lesson Notes for *Rain Forest Animals*

Review vocabulary
Before discussing the article, review any troublesome words with students. First, have students identify words they found difficult to pronounce or to understand. These might include *peccary* (PEK–uh–ree) and *mimicry* (MIM–ih–kree).

Then have students turn to the glossary on page 31 in their books. Review these words with students, pronouncing them and discussing meaning as needed.

See pages 22–25 for strategies for ELL students.

Discuss the informational article
Ask such questions as:

What do you think this article is mostly about?
What information was new or most interesting?
Were you surprised by anything you learned?

Briefly discuss students' responses to the article.

Discuss comprehension questions
After discussing students' responses to the article, discuss the following specific content questions. For each question, have students support their answers by reading relevant sections from the text.

Key Concept 1
- *How would you describe a rain forest habitat?*
- *What are the different levels of a rain forest? Why are these levels important to rain forest animals?*
- *What is a rain forest community? Give examples.*

Key Concept 2
- *What is an example of a rain forest animal that gets what it needs from the rain forest habitat?*
- *How does the animal get what it needs?*

Key Concept 3
- *What is the difference between a physical adaptation and a behavioral adaptation? Provide an example of each.*

41

Essential Core Learning

Every student should have access to the essential literacy, science and social studies content outlined in standards based curriculum. Each of the four books that make up a ***Theme Set*** Unit develops a common set of Key Concepts and core vocabulary. The goal is that each student acquires the same essential information by accessing core content at his or her own reading level.

- The same Key Concepts are developed across all levels.
- All students learn the same Key Vocabulary.
- All students learn the same visual literacy skills.
- All students can contribute to whole class discussions and activities.
- All students learn and apply the same comprehension strategy.
- All students extend their learning as they research and write.
- All students learn about a variety of genres and forms.

By focusing on essential skills and knowledge, students will be able to recall and understand the important elements of the subject they are learning about.

Differentiated Reading

All students should be given the opportunity to access the content at their own level of readiness and ability. The four Student Books in each ***Theme Set*** provide the same critical core content at four different reading levels. The teacher now has materials for struggling readers through fluent readers in her class. Each book presents the material in a variety of ways. By using the text, pictures, and charts, students have several access points to develop their understanding of the material.

Each ***Theme Set*** is accompanied by a comprehensive Teacher's Guide that builds on the best practices in education. The activities vary in complexity, allowing access for all students. Fluent readers are encouraged to work on their own. Readers who need extra help are provided with more scaffolding. Examples of scaffolding used in the **Theme Sets** include explicit instruction, modeling, guided practice, and independent practice.

The Theme Sets vary across levels by

- **increasing the text load and using more complex sentence structure as levels become more challenging.**
- **including vocabulary that grows from simple language to increasingly more difficult words.**
- **expanding concept load as the levels become more challenging.**
- **developing Key Concepts visually as well as verbally.**
- **providing additional picture support at the easier levels.**

Research-Based Instruction

The **Theme Sets** program incorporates best practices that have been identified through research. Practices critical to success in reading and comprehension are highlighted below, as well as ways that the **Theme Sets** support these practices.

Differentiation

"Students who are the same age differ in their readiness to learn, their interests, their styles of learning, their experiences, and their life circumstances."

(Reconcilable Differences? Standards-Based Teaching and Differentiation. Carol Ann Tomlinson. Educational Leadership, Sept. 2000)

- The **Theme Sets** program teaches the same critical core content to every student from struggling to fluent readers.
- Each theme includes four high-interest topics allowing teachers to group their students by reading ability or by interest in the topic.

Appropriate Reading Level

"Effective teachers provide their readers with practice reading materials at their appropriate reading level."

(The Rand Report p.43)

- The **Theme Sets** program provides equal access to science and social studies content for all students at varying reading levels.

Reading in the Content Area

"Teachers who provide comprehension strategy instruction that is deeply connected within the context of subject matter learning, such as history and science, foster comprehension development."

(The Rand Report p.39)

- Each ***Theme Set*** explores a core area of science or social studies content. Students learn strategies to help them access and comprehend the content as they work through the lessons.

Comprehension

"Text comprehension can be improved by instruction that helps readers use specific comprehension strategies."

(Put Reading First p.49)

- Each ***Theme Set*** focuses on one of these six reading comprehension strategies: making connections, asking questions, visualizing, making inferences, determining importance, and synthesizing.

Vocabulary

"Students learn vocabulary directly when they are explicitly taught both individual words and word-learning strategies. Direct vocabulary instruction aids reading comprehension."

(Put Reading First p.35)

- Each ***Theme Set*** has key words that are explicitly taught to all students.
- Each Student Book contains book-level vocabulary words. These words are explicitly taught and repeated often in the text.
- Students are encouraged to use word learning strategies such as context clues and using word parts to determine meaning.

Fluency

"Repeated and monitored oral reading improves reading fluency and overall reading achievement."

(Put Reading First p.24)

- The instructional design of the **THEME SETS** program allows students to repeat reading. The lessons allow time to monitor students' progress.

Genres and Forms

"Students who are aware of text structure organize the text as they read, and they recognize and retain the important information it contains."

(The Rand Report p.40)

- The **THEME SETS** program identifies the characteristics of the major nonfiction genres and forms. These help students develop an understanding of the framework, or schema, for the genre so that new information can be remembered.

Factors Affecting Readability

Teachers can choose from a variety of readability criteria to help make good judgments in choosing appropriate books for students. Yet, as helpful as these criteria might be, no one variable can provide a complete picture of text difficulty.

The four books in each ***Theme Set*** are designed to address the different reading levels within most classrooms. While the Key Concepts are the same across all levels, the texts have been crafted to address the developmental reading needs of a wide range of students.

In determining text difficulty, numerous variables were considered, including nonfiction vocabulary, sentence complexity, concept density, concept complexity, and text density.

Vocabulary	• Vocabulary growth moves from words that are easy, familiar, highly frequent, and usually short, to words that are less common, less frequent,and more abstract or technical. • Multisyllabic words increase as texts become more challenging. • The number of content words highlighted and included in the glossary increases across levels.
Sentence Complexity	• Sentence structure moves from simple, predictable language patterns to more complex patterns with more embedded ideas. • Sentence length increases as levels become more challenging.
Concept Density	• The three Key Concepts in each theme are developed in all levels. • Additional related concepts expand the Key Concepts as the books become more challenging.
Concept Complexity	• Ideas are carefully developed across all levels, but greater prior knowledge is assumed at the more challenging levels. • Concept development at more challenging levels requires more analysis and critical abilities.
Text Density	• The amount of text per page and the length of paragraphs generally increase as books become more challenging. • Easier, more familiar topics, such as animals, may include less text than abstract, less familiar topics, such as energy.

from Level A, *Forest Animals*

Key Concept 2 There are many different habitats on Earth. Animals live in habitats that meet their needs.

What Every Animal Needs

Animals live in habitats that meet their needs. That means that animals live in places where they find shelter. Animals live in places where they can find food and water. They live in places where there is **oxygen**. That is why a temperate forest is a good habitat for many animals.

Food Turtles eat insects and fruit.

Water Bears drink water from rivers and streams.

Shelter Raccoons live in hollow trees.

11

from Level D, *Rain Forest Animals*

Key Concept 2 There are many different habitats on Earth. Animals live in habitats that meet their needs.

What Every Animal Needs

Like all animals on Earth, rain forest animals need to have their basic needs fulfilled. They need food, shelter, water, and oxygen for survival. They find all of these things in their rain forest habitats.

In the rain forest, the mixture of rain and heat creates an ideal place for plants to grow. Trees flower and produce seeds all year round. The variety of plant life provides food for many kinds of animals. Some birds, bats, and insects eat only fruit and flower nectar. Other animals, such as sloths and monkeys, eat leaves. The plant-eating animals may, in turn, become food for meat-eating animals. These include jaguars and anacondas.

Finding water is not hard in the rain forest. In such a wet habitat, rivers, streams, and lush plants provide all the water the animals need.

The thick canopy and dense ground **foliage** of the rain forest shelter many creatures. They help them hide from enemies. Some species have special colors or patterns that help them hide in their plant shelters.

Millions of leaf cutter ants live on the forest floor. They use leaves to grow a special fungus for food.

11

Comparing the Levels

- **Vocabulary becomes more challenging.**
- **Sentences become more complex.**
- **Same Key Concepts but additional related concepts included in more challenging levels.**
- **Concept development at more challenging levels requires more critical thinking.**
- **Text load increases.**

Placing Students in Levels

Matching books to readers is critical in any successful reading program. Selecting books that students can read and want to read involves ongoing assessment of students' reading abilities, an awareness of students' interests, and the ability to judge the difficulty levels of texts.

Student Reading Ability

Use the assessment tools and student records available in your school district as one source of information to determine a student's individual reading level. Consider also students' reading habits, self-selected reading books, and other information in students' reading portfolios. If you are unsure of the ***Theme Set*** level a student should be reading, you can have a student read the first hundred words to you orally. If the student reads with less than 90 percent accuracy, place the student in an easier level. If the student reads with 95 percent or greater accuracy, place the student in a more difficult level. Reassess student placement periodically.

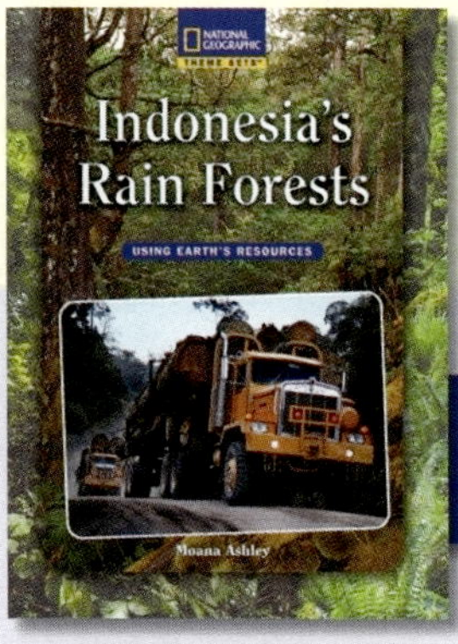

Level A
Fry score 3.2

Use Level A with

- **students who are reading well below grade level.**
- **students who generally have limited vocabulary and background knowledge.**
- **students who generally are most successful with familiar words that are easy to decode and within their oral vocabulary.**
- **students who are most successful with text that uses short and simple sentence structures with straightforward syntax.**
- **students who understand content best when the text uses concrete examples to explain concepts.**
- **students with reading levels that range from 2.6 to 3.5.**

Level B
Fry score 4.4

Use Level B with

- **students who are reading at or below grade level.**
- **students who can read two-syllable words that are easy to decode and within their oral vocabulary.**
- **students who best understand text that uses mostly short, simple sentences with straightforward syntax.**
- **students who understand concepts that are explained carefully and use some concrete examples.**
- **students with reading levels that range from 3.5 to 4.5.**

Student Interest and Motivation

Students who are particularly interested in a topic often bring rich background knowledge to that topic. They are motivated to read more about the topic. This prior knowledge and motivation can allow readers to stretch beyond their overall reading level. In assigning books to students, consider special interest and knowledge. Some students may be interested in reading about a topic in a ***Theme Set*** that is above their reading ability. Provide these students with additional scaffolding and support before, during, and after reading.

Theme Set Reading Levels

The four books in each ***Theme Set*** provide a range of reading levels to facilitate differentiated instruction. However, while Levels A and B are written for struggling readers, they do not look like typical easy-to-read texts. Because of the importance for students to read and learn critical content vocabulary, grade-level content vocabulary was used in Levels A and B. This critical vocabulary was then surrounded by easy-to-read text. Use these guidelines to match students with levels.

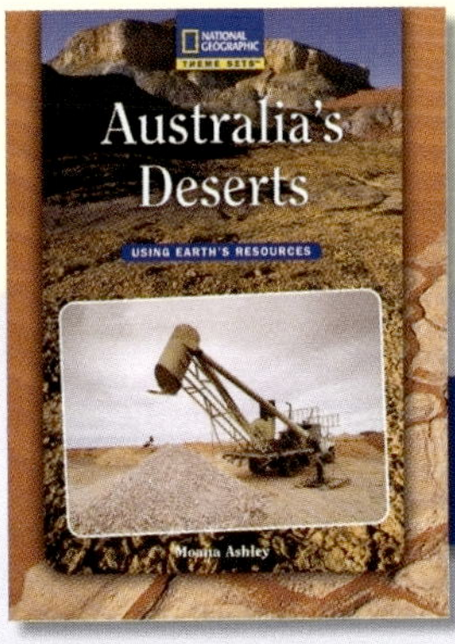

Level C
Fry score 5.5

Use Level C with

- **students who are reading at or above grade level.**
- **students who have a good grasp of common vocabulary and are able to use context and other resources to unlock the meaning of technical content words.**
- **students who can understand simple and most complex sentence structures.**
- **students who, with appropriate support, can understand abstract concepts.**
- **students with reading levels that range from 4.8 to 5.9.**

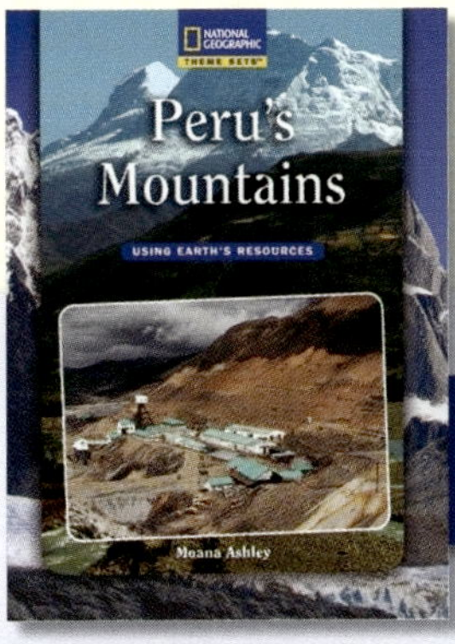

Level D
Fry score 6.8

Use Level D with

- **students who are your strongest readers.**
- **students who have well-developed vocabularies and broad background knowledge about a range of topics.**
- **students who are able to understand most complex sentence structures used in expository writing.**
- **students who can grasp abstract concepts with appropriate support.**
- **students with reading levels that range from 6.0 to 6.9.**

Supporting English Language Learners

To be successful in mainstream classrooms, students acquiring English need to learn grade-level content as they learn language. The **THEME SETS** provide all students with access to grade-level content in science and social studies while supporting the development of language and literacy skills. The unique instructional design of the **THEME SETS** supports English Language Learners by providing the strategies and scaffolding they need.

Scaffold the Content

Target Key Concepts

English Language Learners benefit from instruction that isolates and makes explicit the big ideas of the lesson. Key Concepts are highlighted on the pages and taught through concrete examples and visuals.

Develop Key Vocabulary

English Language Learners need to build their academic vocabulary to access grade-level content. In the **THEME SETS**, Key Vocabulary is highlighted in the text and defined on the page. Key Vocabulary is repeated frequently.

Provide strong picture support

Striking National Geographic photos and illustrations support the text and concepts in comprehensive ways.

Develop visual literacy skills

Lessons in visual literacy offer explicit instruction on how to understand and interpret information presented in diagrams, maps, charts, and other visuals.

Scaffold the Instruction

Build background

Background knowledge for Key Concepts is carefully developed in the Student Books to ensure that students understand the big ideas.

Activate prior knowledge

The lesson notes for each theme provide detailed suggestions for connecting what students already know to what they are learning.

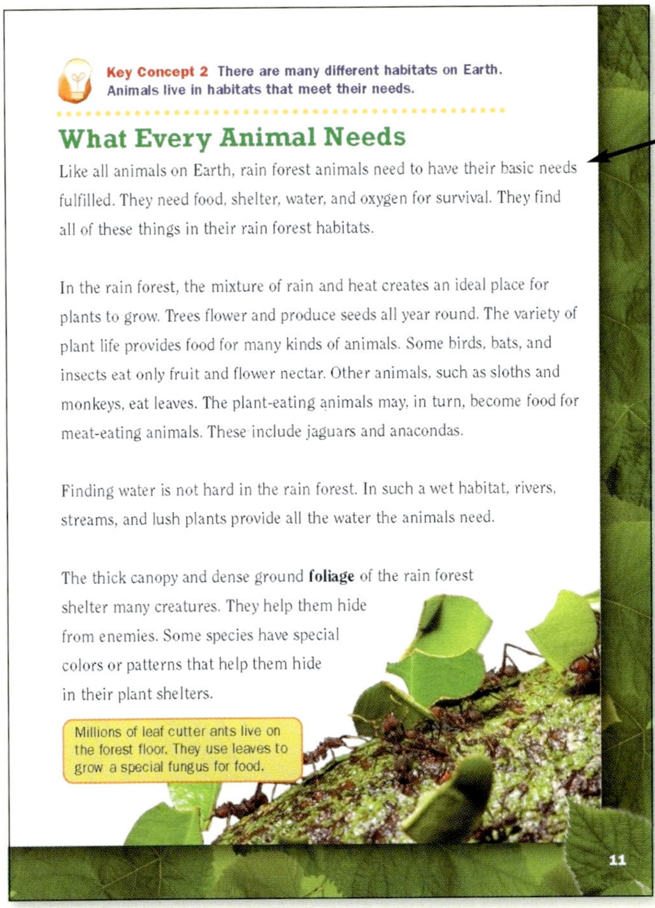

Key Concept 2 There are many different habitats on Earth. Animals live in habitats that meet their needs.

What Every Animal Needs

Like all animals on Earth, rain forest animals need to have their basic needs fulfilled. They need food, shelter, water, and oxygen for survival. They find all of these things in their rain forest habitats.

In the rain forest, the mixture of rain and heat creates an ideal place for plants to grow. Trees flower and produce seeds all year round. The variety of plant life provides food for many kinds of animals. Some birds, bats, and insects eat only fruit and flower nectar. Other animals, such as sloths and monkeys, eat leaves. The plant-eating animals may, in turn, become food for meat-eating animals. These include jaguars and anacondas.

Finding water is not hard in the rain forest. In such a wet habitat, rivers, streams, and lush plants provide all the water the animals need.

The thick canopy and dense ground **foliage** of the rain forest shelter many creatures. They help them hide from enemies. Some species have special colors or patterns that help them hide in their plant shelters.

Millions of leaf cutter ants live on the forest floor. They use leaves to grow a special fungus for food.

11

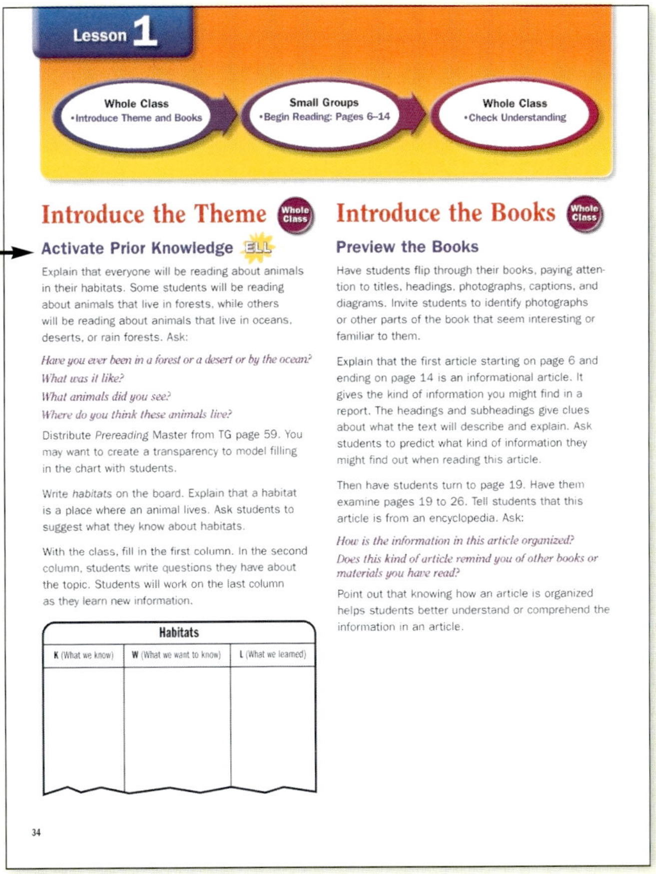

Lesson 1

Whole Class
• Introduce Theme and Books

Small Groups
• Begin Reading: Pages 6–14

Whole Class
• Check Understanding

Introduce the Theme (Whole Class)

Activate Prior Knowledge (ELL)

Explain that everyone will be reading about animals in their habitats. Some students will be reading about animals that live in forests, while others will be reading about animals that live in oceans, deserts, or rain forests. Ask:

Have you ever been in a forest or a desert or by the ocean?
What was it like?
What animals did you see?
Where do you think these animals live?

Distribute *Prereading* Master from TG page 59. You may want to create a transparency to model filling in the chart with students.

Write *habitats* on the board. Explain that a habitat is a place where an animal lives. Ask students to suggest what they know about habitats.

With the class, fill in the first column. In the second column, students write questions they have about the topic. Students will work on the last column as they learn new information.

Habitats

K (What we know)	W (What we want to know)	L (What we learned)

Introduce the Books (Whole Class)

Preview the Books

Have students flip through their books, paying attention to titles, headings, photographs, captions, and diagrams. Invite students to identify photographs or other parts of the book that seem interesting or familiar to them.

Explain that the first article starting on page 6 and ending on page 14 is an informational article. It gives the kind of information you might find in a report. The headings and subheadings give clues about what the text will describe and explain. Ask students to predict what kind of information they might find out when reading this article.

Then have students turn to page 19. Have them examine pages 19 to 26. Tell students that this article is from an encyclopedia. Ask:

How is the information in this article organized?
Does this kind of article remind you of other books or materials you have read?

Point out that knowing how an article is organized helps students better understand or comprehend the information in an article.

34

Beaver Lodge

What's Inside?

Read the diagram by following the steps on page 16. Write down all the things you found out about a beaver lodge. Share what you found out with a classmate. Compare what you learned. What is the same? What is different?

Supporting English Language Learners

Scaffold the Instruction

Teach comprehension strategies

The **Theme Sets** program helps students develop those learning strategies that empower students to become more independent and self-directed in their learning. Each theme provides explicit instruction and practice in one comprehension strategy. Graphic organizers help students use the strategy to understand the content.

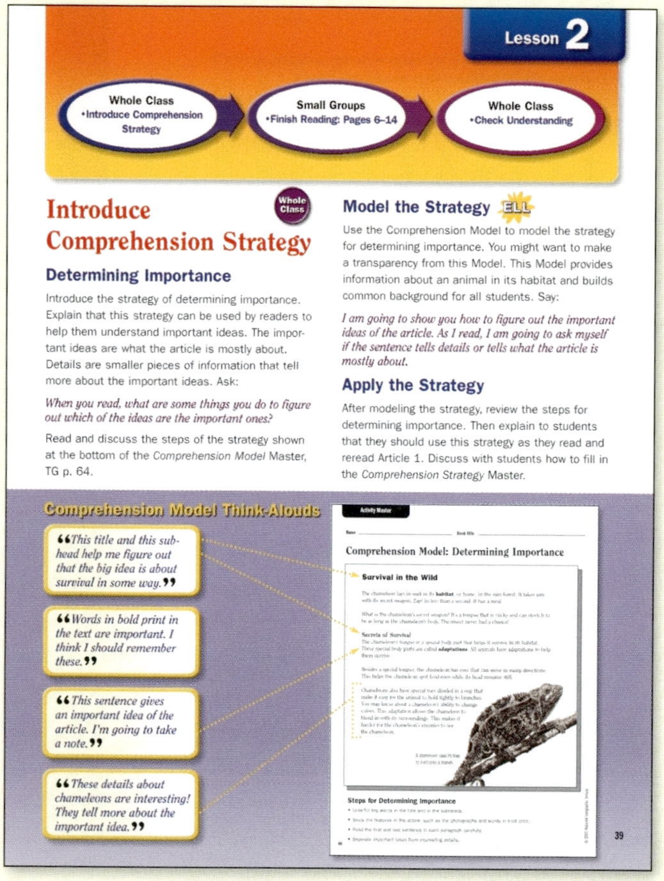

Lesson 2

Whole Class •Introduce Comprehension Strategy | Small Groups •Finish Reading: Pages 6–14 | Whole Class •Check Understanding

Introduce Comprehension Strategy (Whole Class)

Determining Importance

Introduce the strategy of determining importance. Explain that this strategy can be used by readers to help them understand important ideas. The important ideas are what the article is mostly about. Details are smaller pieces of information that tell more about the important ideas. Ask:

When you read, what are some things you do to figure out which of the ideas are the important ones?

Read and discuss the steps of the strategy shown at the bottom of the *Comprehension Model* Master, TG p. 64.

Model the Strategy ELL

Use the Comprehension Model to model the strategy for determining importance. You might want to make a transparency from this Model. This Model provides information about an animal in its habitat and builds common background for all students. Say:

I am going to show you how to figure out the important ideas of the article. As I read, I am going to ask myself if the sentence tells details or tells what the article is mostly about.

Apply the Strategy

After modeling the strategy, review the steps for determining importance. Then explain to students that they should use this strategy as they read and reread Article 1. Discuss with students how to fill in the *Comprehension Strategy* Master.

Comprehension Model Think-Alouds

"This title and this subhead help me figure out that the big idea is about survival in some way."

"Words in bold print in the text are important. I think I should remember these."

"This sentence gives an important idea of the article. I'm going to take a note."

"These details about chameleons are interesting! They tell more about the important idea."

Activity Master

Comprehension Model: Determining Importance

Survival in the Wild

Secrets of Survival

Steps for Determining Importance

39

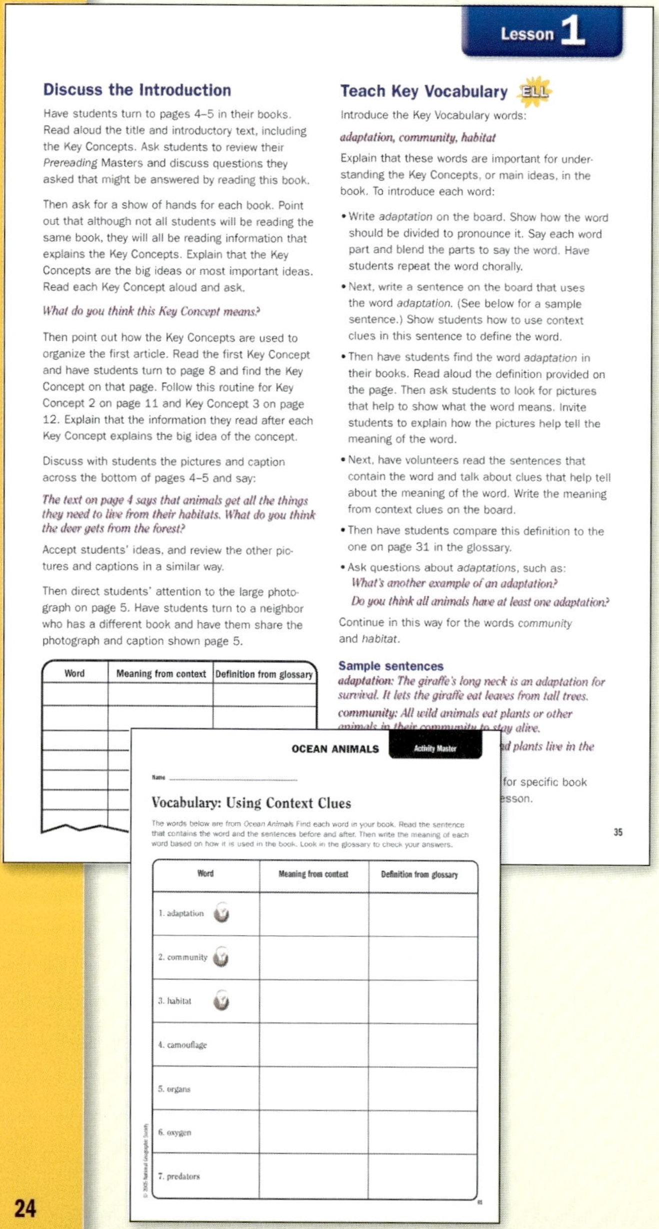

Lesson 1

Discuss the Introduction

Have students turn to pages 4–5 in their books. Read aloud the title and introductory text, including the Key Concepts. Ask students to review their *Prereading* Masters and discuss questions they asked that might be answered by reading this book.

Then ask for a show of hands for each book. Point out that although not all students will be reading the same book, they will all be reading information that explains the Key Concepts. Explain that the Key Concepts are the big ideas or most important ideas. Read each Key Concept aloud and ask.

What do you think this Key Concept means?

Then point out how the Key Concepts are used to organize the first article. Read the first Key Concept and have students turn to page 8 and find the Key Concept on that page. Follow this routine for Key Concept 2 on page 11 and Key Concept 3 on page 12. Explain that the information they read after each Key Concept explains the big idea of the concept.

Discuss with students the pictures and caption across the bottom of pages 4–5 and say:

The text on page 4 says that animals get all the things they need to live from their habitats. What do you think the deer gets from the forest?

Accept students' ideas, and review the other pictures and captions in a similar way.

Then direct students' attention to the large photograph on page 5. Have students turn to a neighbor who has a different book and have them share the photograph and caption shown page 5.

Word	Meaning from context	Definition from glossary

Teach Key Vocabulary ELL

Introduce the Key Vocabulary words:

adaptation, community, habitat

Explain that these words are important for understanding the Key Concepts, or main ideas, in the book. To introduce each word:

- Write *adaptation* on the board. Show how the word should be divided to pronounce it. Say each word part and blend the parts to say the word. Have students repeat the word chorally.
- Next, write a sentence on the board that uses the word *adaptation*. (See below for a sample sentence.) Show students how to use context clues in this sentence to define the word.
- Then have students find the word *adaptation* in their books. Read aloud the definition provided on the page. Then ask students to look for pictures that help to show what the word means. Invite students to explain how the pictures help tell the meaning of the word.
- Next, have volunteers read the sentences that contain the word and talk about clues that help tell about the meaning of the word. Write the meaning from context clues on the board.
- Then have students compare this definition to the one on page 31 in the glossary.
- Ask questions about *adaptations*, such as:
  What's another example of an adaptation?
  Do you think all animals have at least one adaptation?

Continue in this way for the words *community* and *habitat*.

Sample sentences

adaptation: The giraffe's long neck is an adaptation for survival. It lets the giraffe eat leaves from tall trees.

community: All wild animals eat plants or other animals in their community to stay alive.

...*d plants live in the*

...for specific book ...esson.

35

OCEAN ANIMALS Activity Master

Name

Vocabulary: Using Context Clues

The words below are from *Ocean Animals* Find each word in your book. Read the sentence that contains the word and the sentences before and after. Then write the meaning of each word based on how it is used in the book. Look in the glossary to check your answers.

Word	Meaning from context	Definition from glossary
1. adaptation		
2. community		
3. habitat		
4. camouflage		
5. organs		
6. oxygen		
7. predators		

Focus on vocabulary

Rapid vocabulary acquisition is critical to academic success for English Language Learners. Not only do English Language Learners need to close the initial vocabulary gap with native speakers, but they must also keep pace with native speakers by steadily expanding their vocabularies. The **Theme Sets** program offers a rich array of instructional opportunities for English Language Learners to acquire academic vocabulary. These include:

Preteach Vocabulary Key Vocabulary is explicitly taught before reading.

Provide a Rich Context for Words New words are embedded in rich context to ensure that students develop a deeper understanding of these words.

Multiple Exposures and Opportunities to Use Words
The text of the **Theme Sets** is carefully crafted to ensure repeated use of Key Vocabulary so students see words used in different contexts. Throughout the lessons, students are engaged in activities and games that provide rich opportunities to explore and use new vocabulary words.

Provide for Different Proficiency Levels

The English Language Learners in your class may be at different stages of acquiring English. In accommodating these stages, consider adjusting instruction to provide comprehensible input. Vary student response modes to ensure that all students can participate.

The following descriptions of language acquisition stages are summarized from *Sheltered Content Instruction: Teaching English Language Learners with Diverse Abilities* by Jana Echevarria and Anne Graves (Boston: Allyn & Bacon, 2003), pages 15–19.

Preproduction Level	These students benefit from activities that build listening comprehension and receptive vocabulary while allowing them to respond through nonverbal means. They know almost no vocabulary in English. They communicate with gestures, actions, and a few words. They are building their receptive vocabulary and may experience a "silent period" as they attempt to process the tremendous amount of new information about language, culture, and school.
Early Production	These students benefit from lessons that continue to build vocabulary while encouraging them to produce previously learned language. Students can use one-word and two-word responses and chunks of language, drawing upon an English vocabulary of about a thousand words. They can answer who, what, and where questions with brief responses, and can label and categorize information in English. They communicate more readily in English but may experience "adaptation fatigue" as their frustrations with the new language and culture come to a peak.
Speech Emergence	Students use language purposefully and produce complete sentences. They can successfully participate in English in small-group activities. They may feel continued frustration or experience relief as their knowledge base in English expands. They may actually make more errors as they experiment with more complex language patterns. They may feel conflicted about their cultural identity as they adjust to a new language and cultural environment. They benefit from activities that expand vocabulary and promote higher levels of language use.
Intermediate Fluency	Students can read and write in English and have strong conversational skills. They can produce connected narratives and respond to higher level questions, with errors that are usually in style or usage. They may lag behind in academic tasks, however, especially if they lack academic skills in the home language. They benefit from direct instruction of study skills and learning strategies and from strong contextual support for academic tasks.
Advanced Fluency	These students have become fluent speakers, readers, and writers of English. They can participate fully in classroom activities but may still have gaps in certain academic areas. They will benefit from explicit strategy instruction and continued affirmation of their home cultures.

Assessing Progress

Assessment provides teachers with valuable information to help plan instruction and measure progress over time. An assessment program needs to be ongoing so that changes over time in students' learning can be noted. An assessment program needs to include both formal and informal tools so that evaluation of performance is reliable and useful.

The **Theme Sets** program helps you informally assess student progress in both content-area knowledge and literacy development. The following informal assessment opportunities are built into each ***Theme Set***.

Student Book Assessment Tools

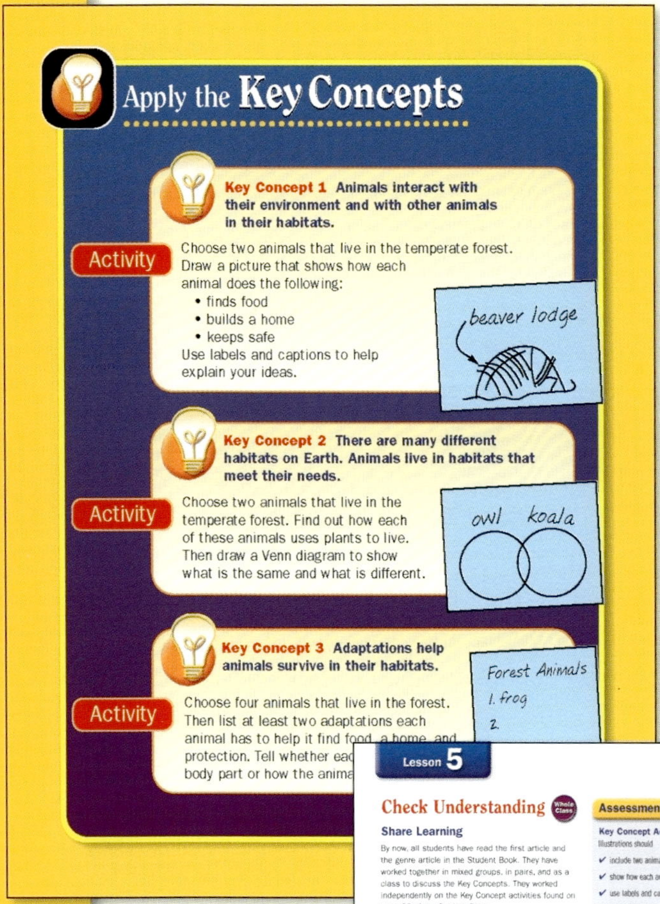

Apply the Key Concepts

Key Concept 1 Animals interact with their environment and with other animals in their habitats.

Activity

Choose two animals that live in the temperate forest. Draw a picture that shows how each animal does the following:
- finds food
- builds a home
- keeps safe

Use labels and captions to help explain your ideas.

Key Concept 2 There are many different habitats on Earth. Animals live in habitats that meet their needs.

Activity

Choose two animals that live in the temperate forest. Find out how each of these animals uses plants to live. Then draw a Venn diagram to show what is the same and what is different.

Key Concept 3 Adaptations help animals survive in their habitats.

Activity

Choose four animals that live in the forest. Then list at least two adaptations each animal has to help it find food, a home, and protection. Tell whether eac... body part or how the anima...

Think About Key Concept Questions At the end of the first informational article in each ***Theme Set***, a common set of questions taps into the students' knowledge of the three Key Concepts. The Teacher's Guide provides an Assessment Check and sample answers for the four books in each theme. See page 44–45.

Key Concept Activities At the end of the second article, in each ***Theme Set***, three activities provide opportunities for students to demonstrate their understanding of the Key Concepts. These activities tap into the various learning styles. The Teacher's Guide provides an Assessment Check to evaluate student products. See page 54.

Research and Write The writing activity that concludes each book allows students to demonstrate what they have learned about the content as well as produce a specific nonfiction writing form. A rubric for evaluating the writing is provided in the Assessment Check in the Teacher's Guide. See page 56.

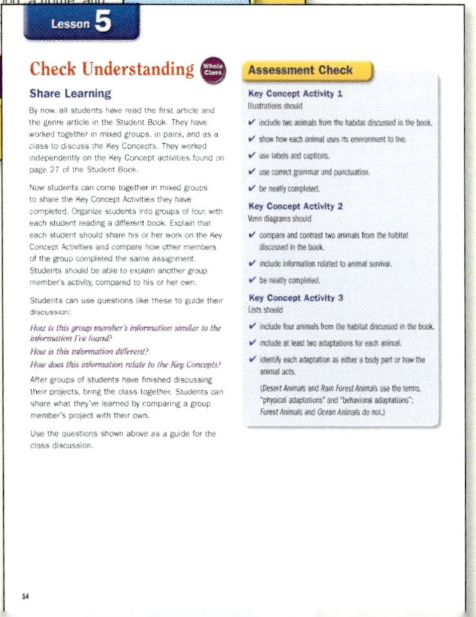

Lesson 5

Check Understanding (Whole Class)

Share Learning

By now, all students have read the first article and the genre article in the Student Book. They have worked together in mixed groups, in pairs, and as a class to discuss the Key Concepts. They worked independently on the Key Concept activities found on page 27 of the Student Book.

Now students can come together in mixed groups to share the Key Concept Activities they have completed. Organize students into groups of four, with each student reading a different book. Explain that each student should share his or her work on the Key Concept Activities and compare how other members of the group completed the same assignment. Students should be able to explain another group member's activity, compared to his or her own.

Students can use questions like these to guide their discussion:

How is this group member's information similar to the information I've found?
How is this information different?
How does this information relate to the Key Concepts?

After groups of students have finished discussing their projects, bring the class together. Students can share what they've learned by comparing a group member's project with their own.

Use the questions shown above as a guide for the class discussion.

Assessment Check

Key Concept Activity 1
Illustrations should
- ✔ include two animals from the habitat discussed in the book.
- ✔ show how each animal uses its environment to live.
- ✔ use labels and captions.
- ✔ use correct grammar and punctuation.
- ✔ be neatly completed.

Key Concept Activity 2
Venn diagrams should
- ✔ compare and contrast two animals from the habitat discussed in the book.
- ✔ include information related to animal survival.
- ✔ be neatly completed.

Key Concept Activity 3
Lists should
- ✔ include four animals from the habitat discussed in the book.
- ✔ include at least two adaptations for each animal.
- ✔ identify each adaptation as either a body part or how the animal acts.

(*Desert Animals* and *Rain Forest Animals* use the terms "physical adaptations" and "behavioral adaptations"; *Forest Animals* and *Ocean Animals* do not.)

54

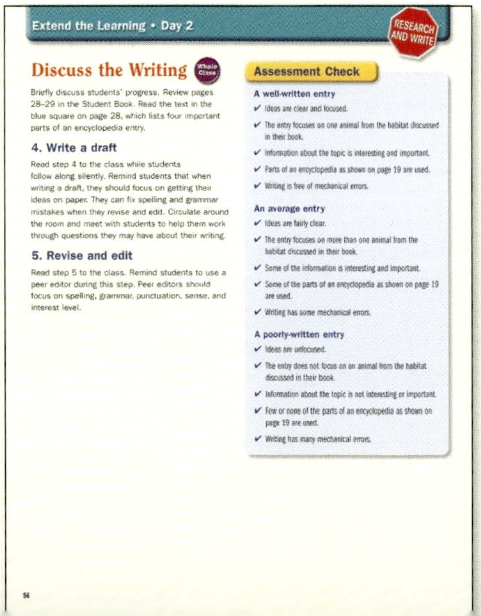

Extend the Learning • Day 2

RESEARCH AND WRITE

Discuss the Writing (Whole Class)

Briefly discuss students' progress. Review pages 28–29 in the Student Book. Read the text in the blue square on page 28, which lists four important parts of an encyclopedia entry.

4. Write a draft

Read step 4 to the class while students follow along silently. Remind students that when writing a draft, they should focus on getting their ideas on paper. They can fix spelling and grammar mistakes when they revise and edit. Circulate around the room and meet with students to help them work through questions they may have about their writing.

5. Revise and edit

Read step 5 to the class. Remind students to use a peer editor during this step. Peer editors should focus on spelling, grammar, punctuation, sense, and interest level.

Assessment Check

A well-written entry
- ✔ Ideas are clear and focused.
- ✔ The entry focuses on one animal from the habitat discussed in their book.
- ✔ Information about the topic is interesting and important.
- ✔ Parts of an encyclopedia as shown on page 19 are used.
- ✔ Writing is free of mechanical errors.

An average entry
- ✔ Ideas are fairly clear.
- ✔ The entry focuses on more than one animal from the habitat discussed in their book.
- ✔ Some of the information is interesting and important.
- ✔ Some of the parts of an encyclopedia as shown on page 19 are used.
- ✔ Writing has some mechanical errors.

A poorly-written entry
- ✔ Ideas are unfocused.
- ✔ The entry does not focus on an animal from the habitat discussed in their book.
- ✔ Information about the topic is not interesting or important.
- ✔ Few or none of the parts of an encyclopedia as shown on page 19 are used.
- ✔ Writing has many mechanical errors.

56

Teacher's Guide Assessment Tools

Open-Book Test In each Teacher's Guide, an Open-Book Test is provided as a blackline master. This test is constructed to help evaluate not only what students have learned but also how effectively students can reread to find specific information. A full answer key is provided for all four books in the theme. See pages 73, and 82–83.

Book Assessment Tests In each Teacher's Guide, a two-page test is provided for each title in the ***Theme Set***. These tests, provided as blackline masters, help to evaluate the content knowledge covered in the theme. The format of the test is similar to the National Assessment of Educational Progress (NAEP) test in that it includes multiple-choice questions, short-constructed responses, and long-constructed responses. A Scoring Guide is provided for each test. See pages 74–81 and 84–87.

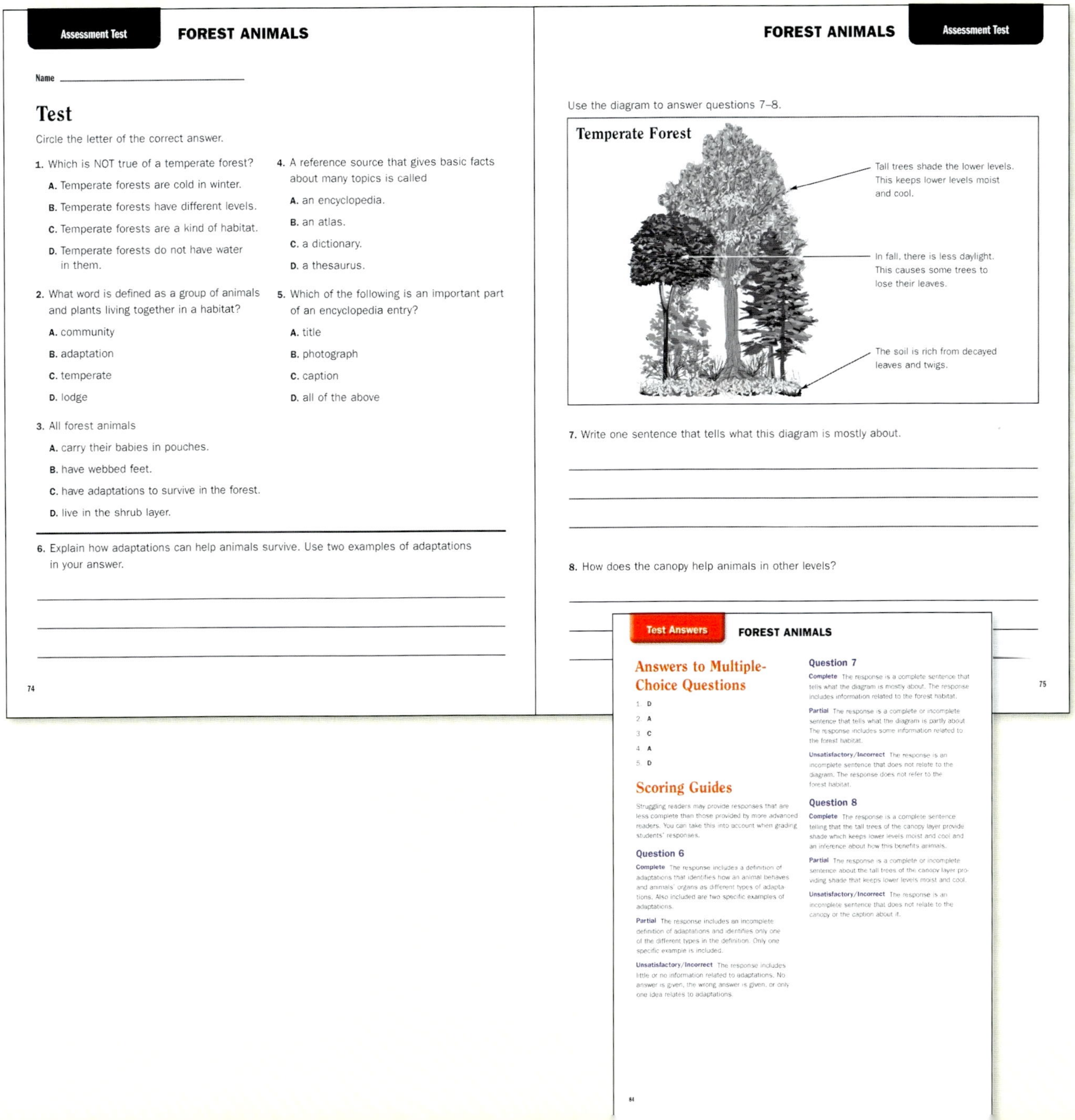

Assessment Test **FOREST ANIMALS**

Name ____________________

Test

Circle the letter of the correct answer.

1. Which is NOT true of a temperate forest?
   - **A.** Temperate forests are cold in winter.
   - **B.** Temperate forests have different levels.
   - **C.** Temperate forests are a kind of habitat.
   - **D.** Temperate forests do not have water in them.
2. What word is defined as a group of animals and plants living together in a habitat?
   - **A.** community
   - **B.** adaptation
   - **C.** temperate
   - **D.** lodge
3. All forest animals
   - **A.** carry their babies in pouches.
   - **B.** have webbed feet.
   - **C.** have adaptations to survive in the forest.
   - **D.** live in the shrub layer.
4. A reference source that gives basic facts about many topics is called
   - **A.** an encyclopedia.
   - **B.** an atlas.
   - **C.** a dictionary.
   - **D.** a thesaurus.
5. Which of the following is an important part of an encyclopedia entry?
   - **A.** title
   - **B.** photograph
   - **C.** caption
   - **D.** all of the above
6. Explain how adaptations can help animals survive. Use two examples of adaptations in your answer.

74

FOREST ANIMALS Assessment Test

Use the diagram to answer questions 7–8.

7. Write one sentence that tells what this diagram is mostly about.
8. How does the canopy help animals in other levels?

75

Test Answers **FOREST ANIMALS**

Answers to Multiple-Choice Questions

1. D
2. A
3. C
4. A
5. D

Scoring Guides

Struggling readers may provide responses that are less complete than those provided by more advanced readers. You can take this into account when grading students' responses.

Question 6

Complete The response includes a definition of adaptations that identifies how an animal behaves and animals' organs as different types of adaptations. Also included are two specific examples of adaptations.

Partial The response includes an incomplete definition of adaptations and identifies only one of the different types in the definition. Only one specific example is included.

Unsatisfactory/Incorrect The response includes little or no information related to adaptations. No answer is given, the wrong answer is given, or only one idea relates to adaptations.

Question 7

Complete The response is a complete sentence that tells what the diagram is mostly about. The response includes information related to the forest habitat.

Partial The response is a complete or incomplete sentence that tells what the diagram is partly about. The response includes some information related to the forest habitat.

Unsatisfactory/Incorrect The response is an incomplete sentence that does not relate to the diagram. The response does not refer to the forest habitat.

Question 8

Complete The response is a complete sentence telling that the tall trees of the canopy layer provide shade which keeps lower levels moist and cool and an inference about how this benefits animals.

Partial The response is a complete or incomplete sentence about the tall trees of the canopy layer providing shade that keeps lower levels moist and cool.

Unsatisfactory/Incorrect The response is an incomplete sentence that does not relate to the canopy or the caption about it.

84

Extend Your Reading

For additional reading, National Geographic provides many related titles to support ***Using Earth's Resources***. Students can use these books for independent reading, for research, or to extend their interest in the subject matter.

Related titles for *Using Earth's Resources*

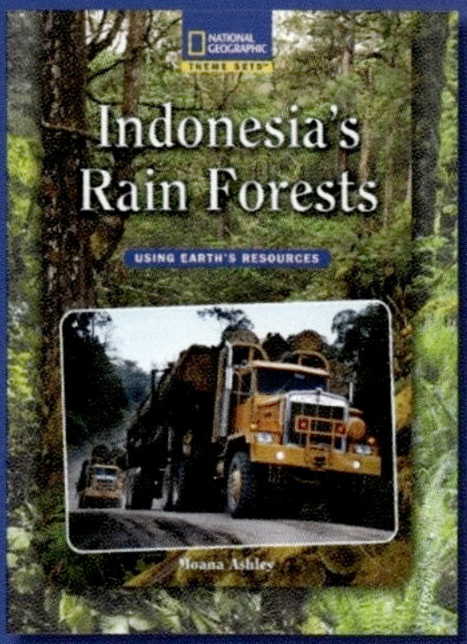

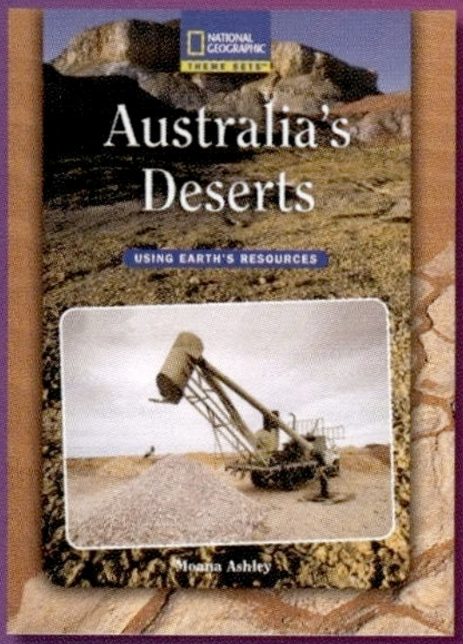

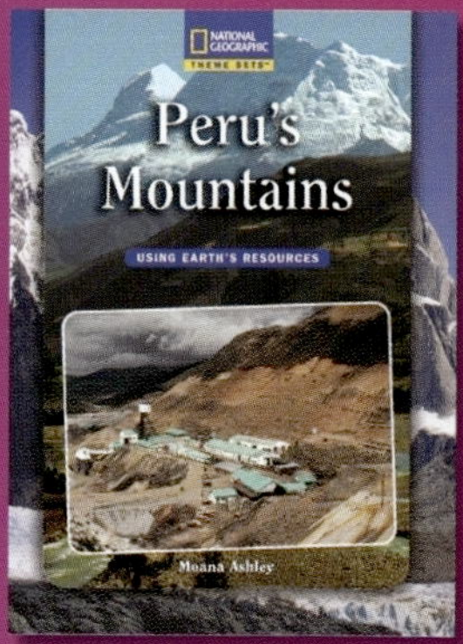

For Research and Further Reading

Windows on Literacy Fluent and Fluent Plus

The Rainforest (Level 18)

Life in the Ocean (Level 18)

Going Up the Mountain (Level 18)

Reading Expeditions

Protecting the Planet (Fry 4.6, Lexile 870, Guided Reading Level T-U)

The Ocean Around Us (Fry 5.5, Lexile 760, Guided Reading Level U-V)

Wonders of Water (Fry 4.7, Lexile 680, Guided Reading Level R-S)

Sylvia Earle: Protecting the Seas (Fry 6.4, Lexile 850, Guided Reading Level X-Y)

Journeying into Rainforests (Fry 4.5, Lexile 600, Guided Reading Level R-S)

Kids Care For the Earth (Fry 5.4, Lexile 650, Guided Reading Level S-T)

Deserts (Fry 3.9, Lexile 630, Guided Reading Level R-S)

Mountains (Fry 570, Lexile 570, Guided Reading Level R-S)

For Reading and Writing Strategies Practice

Nonfiction Reading and Writing Workshops

The comprehension strategy of making inferences is taught in *Using Earth's Resources*. For additional instruction and practice, use the *Making Inferences* titles in the Nonfiction Reading and Writing Workshops.

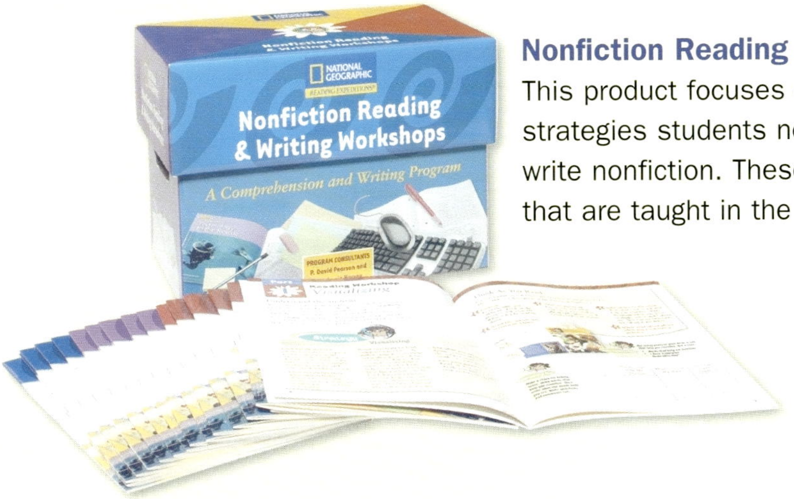

Nonfiction Reading and Writing Workshops

This product focuses on teaching the essential strategies students need to comprehend and write nonfiction. These are the same strategies that are taught in the **THEME SETS** program.

Windows on Literacy Fluent and Fluent Plus

These nonfiction leveled readers are written at the Grade 2–3 level and complement your ***Theme Set*** Level A students.

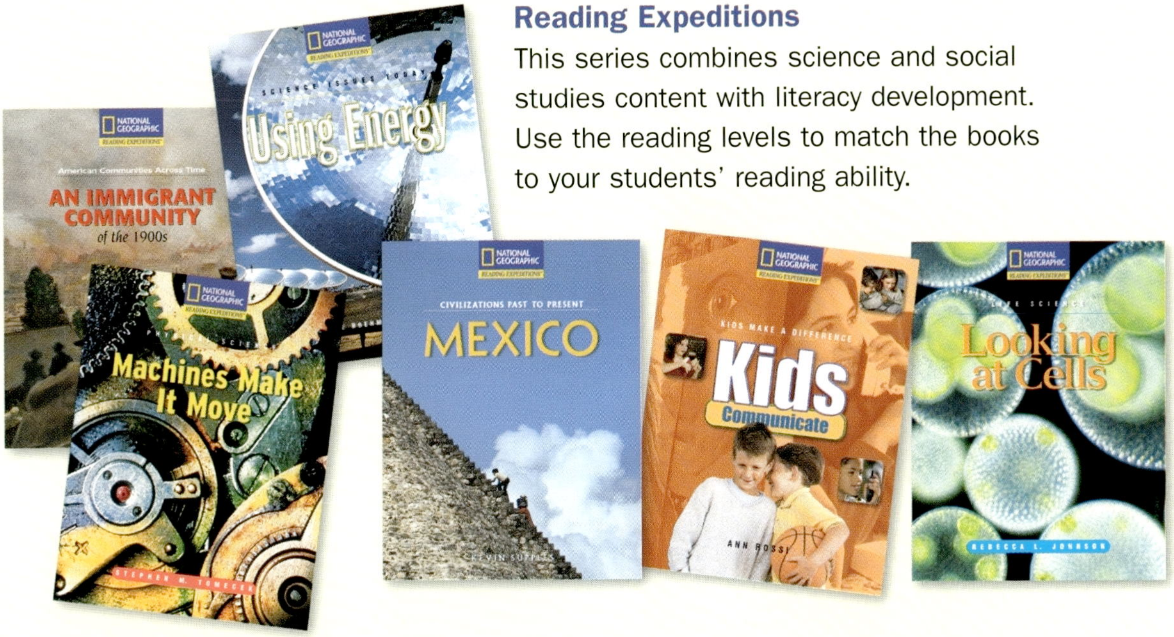

Reading Expeditions

This series combines science and social studies content with literacy development. Use the reading levels to match the books to your students' reading ability.

Theme Overview

Using Earth's Resources

Same in all books

Key Concepts

Key Concept 1:
Key Concept 2:
Key Concept 3:

Key Vocabulary

Literacy Development

Comprehension Strategy
Making Inferences

Varies from book to book

Reading Levels

Least Challenging

Book Vocabulary

Indonesia's Rain Forests

climate
fibers
malaria
nonrenewable
properties
renewable

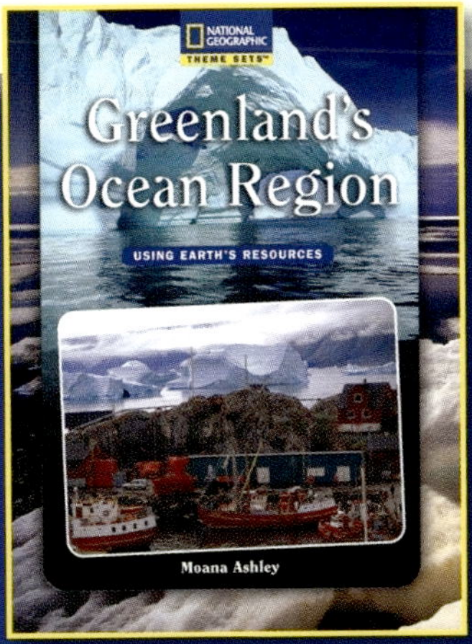

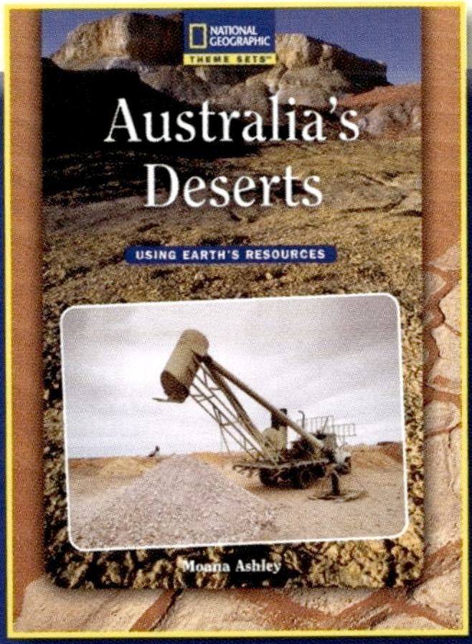

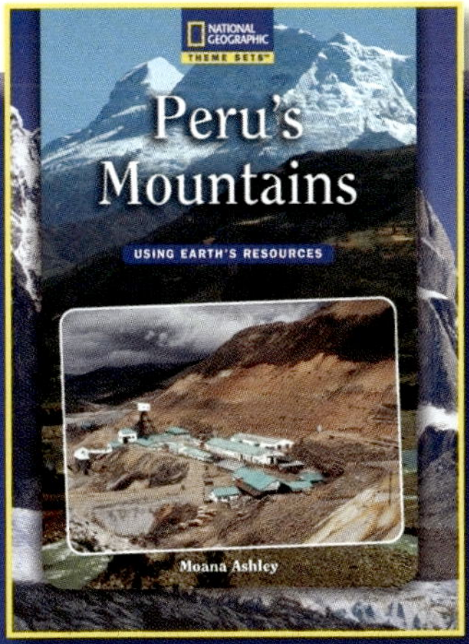

Earth provides many natural resources that people can use.
Different resources are useful to people in different ways.
Conservation and recycling can help save resources.

conservation, natural resources, recycling

Visual Literacy Resource Map
Genre Study Problem-Solution Article

Writing Activity
Write Your Own Problem-Solution Article

As text becomes more challenging:
- Vocabulary and text load increase
- Sentence structure and concepts become more complex

Most Challenging

Greenland's Ocean Region

iron
marine
nonrenewable
nutrients
properties
protein
renewable
vitamin D

Australia's Deserts

coal
conductor
efficiently
exports
fuels
generate
minerals
mining
natural gas
nonrenewable
properties
renewable
rust

Peru's Mountains

alloy
altitudes
conductor
deforestation
depleted
deposits
malleable
minerals
nonrenewable
properties
quinine
renewable
replenished
tropics

Theme Background

Using Earth's Resources explains some of the different regions of Earth, such as rain forests, oceans, deserts, and mountains, from which people collect resources to use. Each book focuses on a different region and the specific resources that come from these areas. However, the same key concepts are developed across books to help students focus on the big ideas.

The theme explores the natural resources Earth provides and how people use these resources. The theme also develops an understanding of how people can help to conserve and recycle to use these resources wisely. Students use the specific content and vocabulary within each book to discuss and examine these big ideas, or Key Concepts.

Each book in this theme includes two articles.

Article 1
Genre: Informational Article Informational articles present information that might be found in a report. Informational articles use headings, subheadings, photographs with labels or captions, boldface words, diagrams, and maps.

Article 2
Genre: Problem-Solution Article This genre enhances students' understanding of the Key Concept statements developed in Article 1. Problem-Solution Articles give information about a problem and possible solutions to that problem. Articles such as these use titles, introductions, body paragraphs, and photographs to inform the reader.

Literacy Objectives

Article 1
Genre: Informational Article

Text features
- headings
- photographs
- captions
- maps

Article 2
Genre: Problem-Solution Article

Text features
- title
- introduction
- photographs
- captions

Comprehension Strategy
Making Inferences

Visual Literacy
Resource Map

Genre Study
Problem-Solution Article

Writing Activity
Write Your Own Problem-Solution Article

Correlation to National Standards

Reading/Language Arts
- Read to be informed
- Apply a wide range of strategies to comprehend and interpret texts
- Use visual and written language to communicate effectively
- Use a variety of informational resources
- Conduct research

Science
- Scientific Inquiry (K–4, 5–8)
- Organisms and their environment (K–4)
- Properties of Earth materials (K–4)
- Types of resources (K–4)
- Science and technology in local challenges (K–4)
- Populations, resources, and environments (5–8)

At a Glance Planner

See Pacing Guide suggestions on pages 12–13.

Pacing Guide	Student Edition Pages	Activity Masters
Lesson 1 • Activate prior knowledge • Preview the theme and books • Discuss Key Vocabulary • Begin reading the first article	***Using Earth's Resources,*** pp. 4–5 **Informational Article,** pp. 6–16	**Prereading:** Word Web TG p. 59 **Vocabulary:** Word Knowledge Chart TG pp. 60–63
Lesson 2 • Teach and apply the comprehension strategy • Finish reading the first article	**Informational Article,** pp. 6–16	**Comprehension Model:** Making Inferences TG p. 64 **Comprehension Strategy:** Making Inferences TG p. 65 **Prereading:** Word Web TG p. 59 **Word Cards:** *Indonesia's Rain Forests* TG p. 66 **Word Cards:** *Greenland's Ocean Region* TG p. 67
Lesson 3 • Discuss and complete the Key Concept questions • Discuss Visual Literacy	**Think About the Key Concepts,** p. 17 **Visual Literacy:** Resource Map, pp. 18–19	**Key Concept Questions** TG p. 69
Lesson 4 • Discuss the Genre Study (Problem-Solution Article) • Begin reading the second article	**Problem-Solution Article,** pp. 20–26	**Fluency Practice** TG p. 70 **Content Reading Guide** TG p. 71
Lesson 5 • Finish reading the second article • Begin Key Concept Activities	**Problem-Solution Article,** pp. 20–26 **Apply the Key Concepts,** p. 27	
Extend the Learning **Day 1** Research and Write **Day 2** Research and Write **Day 3** Sharing Your Work	**Research and Write,** pp. 28–29 **Sharing Your Work,** p. 30	**Prewriting** TG p. 72

Lesson 1

Whole Class
• Introduce Theme and Books

Small Groups
• Begin Reading: Pages 6–16

Whole Class
• Check Understanding

Introduce the Theme (Whole Class)

Activate Prior Knowledge (ELL)

Explain that everyone will be reading about a different area where natural resources are found. Some students will be reading about Indonesia's rain forests, while others will be reading about the oceans around Greenland, Australia's deserts, or Peru's mountains. Ask:

What are some things we get from Earth that we use to live?

What do you think life would be like if Earth did not provide us with these things?

Distribute the *Prereading* Master found in this Teacher's Guide, page 59. You may want to create a transparency to model filling in the Master with students.

Write *natural resources* in the center oval of a word web. Explain that natural resources are useful materials that we find in nature. Ask students to name some natural resources they know. With the class, draw lines from the center oval of the web and write the types of natural resources students name. Students can then name some ways these natural resources are used and add these ideas to the next level of the web. Students will continue to add words to their webs as they learn new information.

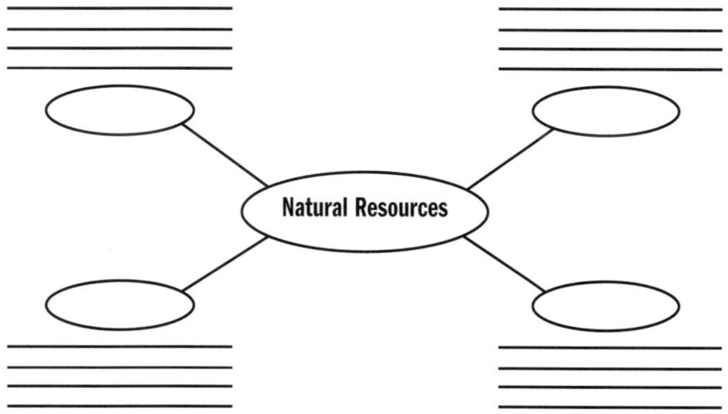

Introduce the Books (Whole Class)

Preview the Books

Have students flip through their books, paying attention to titles, headings, photographs, captions, maps, and labels. Invite students to identify photographs or other parts of the book that seem interesting or familiar to them.

Explain that the first article starting on page 6 and ending on page 16 is an informational article. It gives the kind of information you might find in a report. The headings and subheadings give clues about what the text will describe and explain. Ask students to predict what kind of information they might find out when reading this article.

Then have students turn to page 21. Have them examine pages 21 to 26. Tell students that this article is a problem-solution article. Ask:

How is the information in this article organized?

Does this kind of article remind you of other books or materials you have read?

Point out that knowing how an article is organized helps students better understand the information in an article.

Discuss the Introduction

Have students turn to pages 4–5 in their books. Read aloud the title and introductory text, including the Key Concepts. Ask students to review their *Prereading* Masters and discuss any questions they may have that might be answered by reading this book.

Then ask for a show of hands for each book. Point out that although not all students will be reading the same book, they all will be reading information that explains the Key Concepts. Explain that the Key Concepts are the big ideas or most important ideas. Read each Key Concept aloud and ask:

What do you think this Key Concept means?

Then point out how the Key Concepts are used to organize the first article. Read the first Key Concept and have students turn to page 8 and find the Key Concept on that page. Follow this routine for Key Concept 2 on page 11 and Key Concept 3 on page 14. Explain that the information they read after each Key Concept explains the big idea of the concept.

Discuss with students the pictures and captions across the bottom of pages 4–5 and say:

The text on page 4 says that nature provides people with many useful things. What useful things do you think can be found in rain forests?

Accept students' ideas, and review the other pictures and captions in a similar way.

Then direct students' attention to the large photograph on page 5. Have students turn to a neighbor who has a different book and have them share the photograph and caption shown on page 5.

Word	Know the word well	Have heard the word	Know nothing about the word	Definition

Teach Key Vocabulary ELL

Introduce the Key Vocabulary words:

conservation, natural resources, recycling

Explain that these words are important for understanding the Key Concepts, or main ideas, in the book. To introduce each word:

- Write *conservation* on the board. Show how the word should be divided to pronounce it. Say each word part and blend the parts to say the word. Have students repeat the word chorally.
- Draw a chart with 5 columns on the board. Write the following heads at the top of the columns: Word, Know the word well, Have heard the word, Know nothing about the word, Definition.
- Have students skim the first article to find the word *conservation* in green print on page 8 in the text. Write *conservation* in the first column of the chart.
- Next, ask a volunteer to say whether he or she knows the word well, has heard the word, or knows nothing about the word. Make a check mark in the appropriate box on the chart.
- If the student knows a word well or has heard a word before, have him or her offer a word or two to help define it. Write these words on the chart. If the student gives a definition that is not appropriate for how the word is used in context, comment that some words have several meanings. Have students look up the word in the glossary.
- If there is a word that no students find familiar, ask a volunteer to look the word up in the glossary and then offer words that define it to put on the chart.
- Then ask students to look for pictures in their books that help to show what the word means. Invite students to point to or explain which pictures help them understand the meaning of the word or relate to the word.

Continue on this way for the words *natural resources* and *recycling*.

Students will use this word knowledge chart for specific book vocabulary words later in this Lesson.

Begin Reading: Pages 6–16

Small Groups

	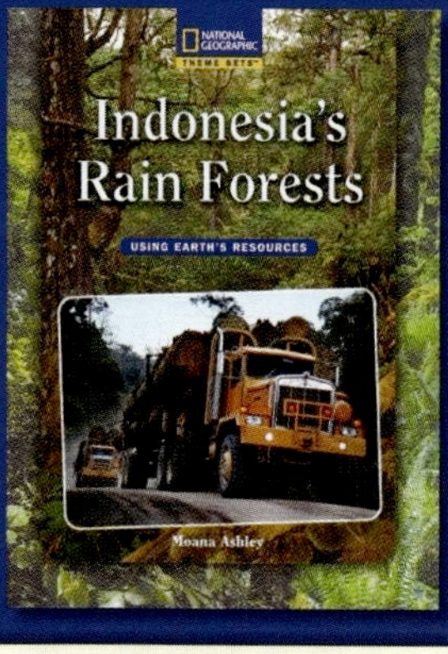		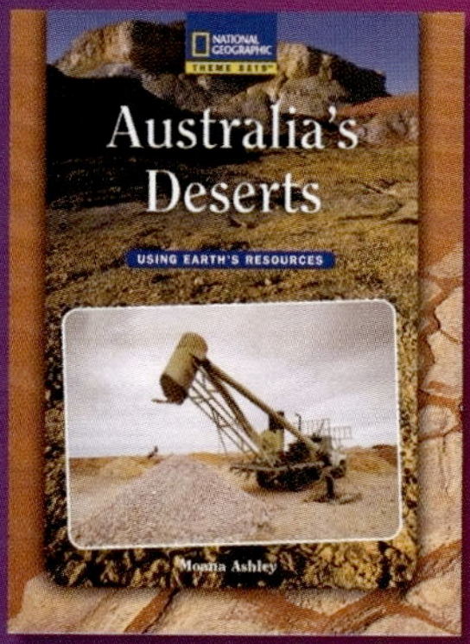	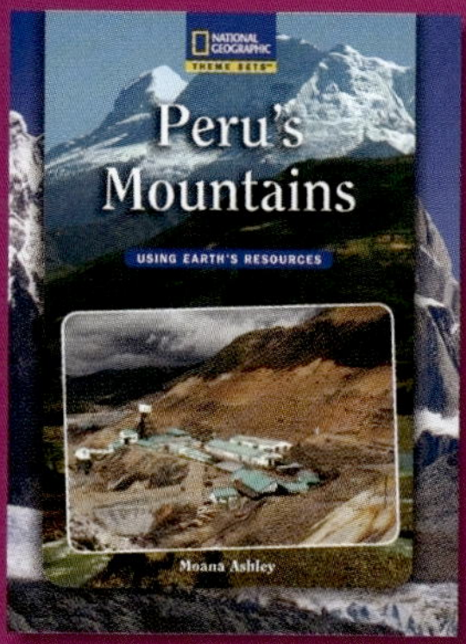
First Activity Block	**With the Teacher** **Begin Reading** • Introduce words difficult for students to read. • Introduce book vocabulary. • Begin reading the article in sections. • Check comprehension following each section.	*Pairs* **Vocabulary** Word Knowledge Chart To each student, distribute the *Greenland's Ocean Region Vocabulary* Master. Students can work in pairs to complete this Master.	*Pairs* **Vocabulary** Word Knowledge Chart To each student, distribute the *Australia's Deserts Vocabulary* Master. Students can work in pairs to complete this Master.	*Pairs* **Vocabulary** Word Knowledge Chart To each student, distribute the *Peru's Mountains Vocabulary* Master. Students can work in pairs to complete this Master.
Second Activity Block	*Pairs* **Vocabulary** Word Knowledge Chart To each student, distribute the *Indonesia's Rain Forests Vocabulary* Master. Students can work in pairs to complete this Master.	**With the Teacher** **Begin Reading** • Introduce words difficult for students to read. • Introduce book vocabulary. • Begin reading the article in sections. • Check comprehension following each section.	*Individuals* **Independent Reading** Students begin reading *Desert Resources*, Student Book pages 6-16. Students can use their *Prereading* Masters to check their ideas, add information, and write questions they may have.	*Individuals* **Independent Reading** Students begin reading *Mountain Resources*, Student Book pages 6-16. Students can use their *Prereading* Masters to check their ideas, add information, and write questions they may have.

With the Teacher | Small Groups | ELL

Lesson Notes for *Indonesia's Rain Forests*

Introduce difficult words

Identify four or five words in the section that may be difficult for students to read. These can include the Key Vocabulary words if needed. Write the words and show students how to find parts of the words that they already know. Sound out the parts they do not know, and blend the parts together.

Introduce vocabulary

Introduce the book vocabulary words. (See the Teaching Notes on the inside front cover of the Student Books.) Use an approach similar to how you introduced the Key Vocabulary words. Have students read the word with you and decide how familiar they are with the word. If they are familiar with it, they can offer a few words to define it. If not, they can look it up in the glossary.

See pages 22–25 for strategies for ELL students.

Begin reading the article in sections

Point out that the article is divided into sections based on the Key Concepts. Have students read each section aloud. Students can read chorally or take turns. Be sure each student follows along when others read. Spend time reviewing the graphic elements (maps, labels, photographs, and captions). After each section, discuss the content and ask comprehension questions such as:

Key Concept 1

- *What natural resources do Indonesia's rain forests provide?*
- *Why are rain forests important to the oxygen cycle?*

Key Concept 2

- *How are the different rain forest trees used?*

Key Concept 3

- *How can people help to conserve the rain forests?*

Encourage students to use vocabulary words in their responses.

With the Teacher | Small Groups | ELL

Lesson Notes for *Greenland's Ocean Region*

Introduce difficult words

Identify four or five words in the section that may be difficult for students to read. These can include the Key Vocabulary words if needed. Write the words and show students how to find parts of the words that they already know. Sound out the parts they do not know, and blend the parts together.

Introduce vocabulary

Have students bring their vocabulary sheets with them to this group. Write one vocabulary word. Have students read the word with you and tell how familiar they are with the word. Have students offer a few words to define it. Correct any misconceptions and, if necessary, have students look it up in the glossary. Continue with other vocabulary words.

See pages 22–25 for strategies for ELL students.

Begin reading the article in sections

Point out that the article is divided into sections based on the Key Concepts. Have students read each section aloud. Students can read chorally or take turns. Be sure each student follows along when others read. Spend time reviewing the graphic elements (maps, labels, photographs, and captions). After each section, discuss the content and ask comprehension questions such as:

Key Concept 1

- *What natural resources are provided by Greenland's ocean region?*
- *Why are oceans important to the water cycle?*

Key Concept 2

- *How are the different ocean resources used?*

Key Concept 3

- *How can people help to conserve the oceans?*

Encourage students to use vocabulary words in their responses.

Check Understanding

Whole Class

Share Learning

By now, all students have read most of the informational article, either independently or in small groups with the teacher.

Bring the class together, and have students share what they learned from the books in this theme. Ask:

What resource area did you read about?

What are some of the resources found there?

How do people use the resources from this area?

What are the big ideas in the article?

Discuss the Key Concepts

ELL

Students reading different books can explain how the Key Concepts apply to the individual topics. With examples about different natural resources, students can begin to see how the same big ideas apply to natural resources in general.

Review the Key Concepts with the class using a chart. Draw a 2-column chart on the board. Title the chart with the name of the region discussed in one of the books. Write the column heads "Natural resource," and "How resource is used" on the chart. Ask a volunteer who read this book to name a natural resource he or she read about in the informational article. Write the name of that resource in the first column. Ask another student who read the same book to tell ways this resource is used. Write this information in the second column on the chart. Ask the class:

What are some ways natural resources can be used?

Continue in this way until a chart is made for each of the four titles. Help students make connections between the big ideas of the theme and each title.

Indonesia's Rain Forests	
Natural resource	**How resource is used**
trees	furniture, boats, food, medicine

Sample chart for Indonesia's Rain Forests

Revisit the *Prereading* Master

Now that students have read most of Article 1, have them revisit the *Prereading* Master they began at the beginning of the Lesson. Students can work in pairs or independently to compare what they have written and to get new ideas to add to their word webs.

Whole Class
- Introduce Comprehension Strategy

Small Groups
- Finish Reading: Pages 6–16

Whole Class
- Check Understanding

Introduce Comprehension Strategy

Whole Class

Making Inferences

Introduce the strategy of making inferences. Explain that readers can use this strategy to help them make sense of what they are reading. Making inferences will make the reading easier to understand. Ask:

When you read something, do you sometimes use clues in the text and what you already know to find a deeper meaning about what you are reading?

Read and discuss the steps of the strategy shown at the bottom of the *Comprehension Model* Master, TG p. 64.

Model the Strategy ELL

Use the Comprehension Model to model the strategy for making inferences. You might want to make a transparency from this Model. This Model provides information about the importance of taking care of Earth and builds common background for all students. Say:

I am going to show you how to make inferences about what you are reading. I am going to stop and think aloud and then think about what I already know.

Apply the Strategy

After modeling the strategy, review the steps for making inferences. Then explain to students that they should use this strategy as they read and reread Article 1. Discuss with students how to practice the comprehension strategy using the *Comprehension Strategy* Master.

Comprehension Model Think-Alouds

"*Since the food and water we need to live comes from Earth, I can infer that it is important to protect Earth.*"

"*This says that trees make the oxygen we need to breathe. I can infer that without trees and plants we would die.*"

"*The word* conservation *has the word* conserve *in it. I know this means to use less of something. I can infer that this means we need to use fewer trees.*"

"*This says that one person produces a large amount of trash. I can infer that we could run out of space for trash if we don't reduce what we produce.*"

Activity Master

Name ______________ Book title ______________

Comprehension Model: Making Inferences

Handle with Care

Save energy! Don't litter! Reduce air pollution! Do these environmental slogans make a difference in protecting the environment? The answer is yes. Even the efforts of one person can help protect our planet.

Plants and animals, including humans, need food and water to survive. These needs are met by the **natural resources** found on Earth. We grow much of our food in the soil of Earth. If soil can be blown or washed away by wind and water, the soil gets damaged and rich farmland can be turned into a desert wasteland. Farmers plant trees and use better farming practices to prevent this from happening.

Trees are also important for the air we breathe. Trees use carbon dioxide and make the oxygen we need to live. Also, when trees are cut down, many plants and animals lose their habitat. The **conservation** of trees is important to protecting the environment.

The average American produces 10 tons of trash in 13 years. This trash ends up in landfills that pollute the water, air, and land. We can also help to protect the environment by **recycling**, reusing, and reducing what we throw away. In fact, about 80 percent of household trash can be recycled. If everyone worked harder to recycle, we could protect the environment.

The trash we produce pollutes water, air, and land.

Steps for Making Inferences
- Ask questions about what you read.
- Study the pictures to get clues about what you are reading.
- Use words, visuals, and what you already know to make inferences.

64

Finish Reading: Pages 6–16

Small Groups

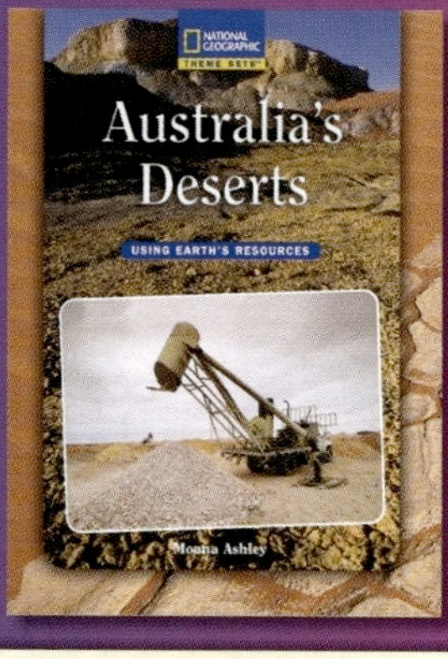

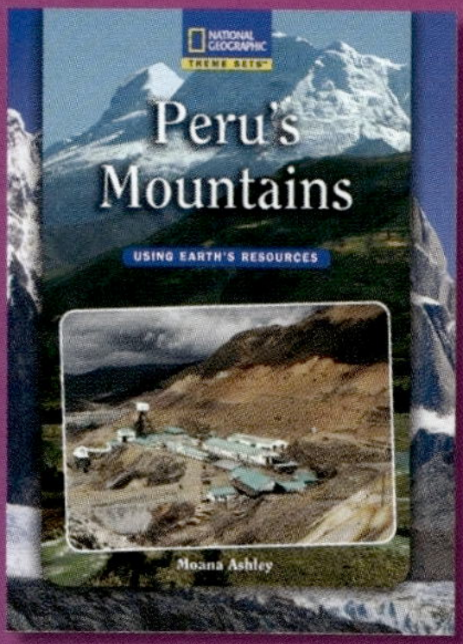

First Activity Block	*Pairs* **Word Card Activity** Pairs of students reading *Indonesia's Rain Forests* can use the word cards found on page 66 of this Teacher's Guide. They can use these word cards to group the words according to different categories. Using these word cards, students gain experience using Key Vocabulary words and vocabulary words for *Indonesia's Rain Forests*.	*Pairs* **Finish Reading/Reread** Students can work with a partner to finish reading *Ocean Resources*, Student Book pages 6-16. Students then reread the article with a partner and complete the *Comprehension Strategy* Master.	**With the Teacher** **Discuss Reading** • Review vocabulary. • Discuss the article. • Discuss comprehension questions.	*Individuals* **Finish Reading/Reread** Students finish reading *Mountain Resources*, Student Book pages 6-16. Students then reread the article and complete the *Comprehension Strategy* Master.
Second Activity Block	*Pairs* **Finish Reading/Reread** Students can work with a partner to finish reading *Rain Forest Resources*, Student Book pages 6-16. Students then reread the article with a partner and complete the *Comprehension Strategy* Master.	*Pairs* **Word Card Activity** Pairs of students reading *Greenland's Ocean Region* can use the word cards found on page 67 of this Teacher's Guide. They can use these word cards to group the words according to different categories. Using these word cards, students gain experience using Key Vocabulary words and vocabulary words for *Greenland's Ocean Region*.	*Individuals* **Finish Reading/Reread** Students finish reading *Desert Resources*, Student Book pages 6-16. Students then reread the article and complete the *Comprehension Strategy* Master.	**With the Teacher** **Discuss Reading** • Review vocabulary. • Discuss the article. • Discuss comprehension questions.

With the Teacher · Small Groups · ELL

Lesson Notes for *Australia's Deserts*

Review vocabulary

Before discussing the article, review any troublesome words with students. First, have students identify words they found difficult to pronounce or to understand.

Then have students turn to the glossary on page 31 in their books. Review these words with students, pronouncing them and discussing meaning as needed.

See pages 22–25 for strategies for ELL students.

Discuss the informational article

Ask questions such as:

What do you think this article is mostly about?

What information was new or most interesting?

Were you surprised by anything you learned?

Briefly discuss students' responses to the article.

Discuss comprehension questions

After discussing students' responses to the article, discuss the following specific content questions. For each question, have students support their answers by reading relevant sections from the text.

Key Concept 1

- *What natural resources do Australia's deserts provide?*
- *How is the rock cycle important for getting coal and natural gas?*

Key Concept 2

- *How are the different resources from the desert used?*

Key Concept 3

- *How can people help conserve desert resources?*

With the Teacher · Small Groups · ELL

Lesson Notes for *Peru's Mountains*

Review vocabulary

Before discussing the article, review any troublesome words with students. First, have students identify words they found difficult to pronounce or to understand. These might include *quisuar* (*kee*-swar) or *quenual* (*kay*-noo-wahl).

Then have students turn to the glossary on page 31 in their books. Review these words with students, pronouncing them and discussing meaning as needed.

See pages 22–25 for strategies for ELL students.

Discuss the informational article

Ask questions such as:

What do you think this article is mostly about?

What information was new or most interesting?

Were you surprised by anything you learned?

Briefly discuss students' responses to the article.

Discuss comprehension questions

After discussing students' responses to the article, discuss the following specific content questions. For each question, have students support their answers by reading relevant sections from the text.

Key Concept 1

- *What natural resources do Peru's mountains provide?*
- *How do the mountains affect the climate of the region?*

Key Concept 2

- *How are the different resources from the mountains used?*

Key Concept 3

- *How can people help conserve mountain resources?*

Check Understanding

Whole Class

Review the Comprehension Strategy

Remind students that when they read, they use different strategies to help them better understand what they read. Review with them the strategy of making inferences.

- **Ask questions about what you read.**
- **Study the pictures to get clues about what you are reading.**
- **Use words, visuals, and what you already know to make inferences.**
- **Look beyond words and pictures to infer what the big idea is.**

Select a sample passage from one of the four books and model thinking aloud as you read the passage. You could also reuse the *Comprehension Model* Master.

Then review with the class their completed *Comprehension Strategy* Master. To begin, have students work in pairs. Suggest that each student review his or her *Comprehension Strategy* Master notes and select one example of an inference he or she made. Ask students to read aloud to their partners the passage that contains the text they used to infer.

After students have practiced thinking aloud to make inferences, ask volunteers to model this process for the class. Be sure to include students who are reading each of the four books.

Comprehension Strategy Tips

Collect ideas about how students can use the comprehension strategy of making inferences in their reading. Record their ideas on chart paper and post the chart so that students can refer to it when they read other informational articles of this kind. Leave some space at the bottom for additional tips as they come up.

Here is a list of tips that the class might include.

Making Inferences

- **Read everything carefully.**
- **Study the pictures to get information that's not in the article.**
- **Ask questions to help you understand what you are reading.**
- **Take what you know and merge it with clues in the text to make a good guess.**
- **Think about what you know and feel about the topic.**
- **Sometimes reading ahead helps you figure things out.**

Whole Class
• Share Learning

Whole Class
• Think About Key Concept Questions

Whole Class
• Visual Literacy

Share Learning

Whole Class

Review the Key Concepts with the class. Remind students that they have all read an article about a different resource area on Earth, and they have all read about the same Key Concepts. Explain that now students can share what they have learned from their books. Say:

First, we will work in small groups to discuss what we learned about Earth's resources. Then we will come together again to share what we learned with the class.

Next, distribute the *Share Learning* Master found on page 68 of this Teacher's Guide. Then organize students into groups of four, with each student reading a different book. Explain that each student is the group's "expert" on his or her book's information. Group members then complete this Activity Master together, as each student contributes ideas to complete the chart.

After groups of students have completed their charts, bring the class together to create a class chart on the board. Students can share what they've learned from their own books as well as from other students in their group. Ask questions to help students make connections to the big ideas among titles.

Resource location	Resources from the area	How resources are used	How resources can be conserved
Rain forests of Indonesia	trees	to get fruits and nuts to eat and wood for building, making paper, and medicines	protect the forests, use less paper, buy fewer wood items, recycle
Oceans of Greenland	marine animals	for food, for fertilizer, and skins for clothing	limit fishing and seal hunting, recycling water
Deserts of Australia	minerals, metals, gemstones, salts, and fuels	for building, making jewelry, electrical wires, and to heat homes	use less electricity, use more efficient heating and cooling systems, recycling
Mountains of Peru	trees, metals, and minerals	to get fruit for food, medicines, wood for building, to make electrical wires and jewelry	protecting forests, recycling copper

Sample answers for one group of students

Assessment Check

Students should conclude that

✔ there are many locations where natural resources are found.

✔ different locations provide different types of resources.

✔ people can use resources in many different ways.

✔ it is important to conserve natural resources.

Lesson 3

Think About Key Concept Questions

Whole Class

Have students turn to page 17 in their Student Books. On this page, all students will find the same four questions relating to the Key Concept statements.

Think About the Key Concepts

1. **Name two or more resources from the country you read about in this book.**
2. **Name at least three ways the natural resources discussed in this book are used.**
3. **Explain the difference between a renewable resource and a nonrenewable resource.**
4. **Give at least two examples of how people can conserve Earth's resources.**

Read the questions to the class, making sure that students understand each question. You might ask volunteers to rephrase the question in their own words, or you might rephrase the questions for students.

Share Learning

Explain to students that they will complete the *Key Concept Questions* Master independently. Then students will come together as a class to share what they have learned. Say:

You have each read an article about an area where natural resources are found. Not everyone has read the same book, but all books have the same Key Concepts. Now, as you complete the Key Concept Questions *Master, think about what you've learned from reading.*

When we come together as a class to discuss the completed Key Concept Questions *Masters, you can compare what you have learned to what others have learned about communities.*

Review the *Key Concept Questions* Master with students, answering any questions they may have.

Assessment Check

Students should address these main ideas in their responses to the Key Concept questions:

1. There are many different resources Earth provides that people can use.
2. Natural resources can be used in many different ways.
3. Some resources are renewable and others are nonrenewable.
4. There are many ways people can help to conserve Earth's resources.

Possible Responses to Key Concept Questions

Indonesia's Rain Forests	Greenland's Ocean Region	Australia's Deserts	Peru's Mountains
1. Name two or more resources from the country you read about in this book.			
trees, plants, and oxygen	fish and other marine animals, and oceans	minerals, metals, such as gold, iron, and copper, opals, salts, coal, and natural gas	trees, gold, copper, silver, lead, and zinc
2. Name at least three ways the natural resources discussed in this book are used.			
to get fruits and nuts to eat and wood for building, making paper, and medicines	for food, skins for clothing, and fertilizer	for building, making jewelry, electrical wires, and to heat homes	to get fruit for food, medicines, wood for building, to make electrical wires and jewelry
3. Explain the difference between a renewable resource and a nonrenewable resource.			
A renewable resource can be replaced by nature. A non-renewable resource does not get replaced and can get used up.	A renewable resource can be replaced by nature. A non-renewable resource does not get replaced and can get used up.	A renewable resource can be replaced by nature. A non-renewable resource does not get replaced and can get used up.	A renewable resource can be replaced by nature. A non-renewable resource does not get replaced and can get used up.
4. Give at least two examples of how people can conserve Earth's resources.			
People can conserve rain forest resources by protecting the forests, using less paper, buying fewer wood items, and recycling.	People can conserve ocean resources by limiting fishing and seal hunting, and recycling water.	People can conserve desert resources by using less electricity, using more efficient heating and cooling systems, and recycling.	People can conserve mountain resources by protecting resource areas and recycling.

Visual Literacy

Whole Class

Resource Map

Have students turn to page 18 in their books. In all books, this page contains the same information about using resource maps, except that the topic of each map is specific to each book. Say:

I am going to read pages 18 and 19 from Indonesia's Rain Forests. *This book shows a resource map of the world's food resources. Since you are not all reading the same book, you do not have the same resource maps on this page. But the information about resource maps is the same.*

After reading the top half of page 18, review the definition of a resource map.

Then read the three steps in the box at the bottom of page 18. After reading the text in the box, have students look back at the resource maps on page 9 of their books. Say:

While you are looking at the resource maps in your specific book, I'm going to look at page 9 in Indonesia's Rain Forests. *We've all seen these resource maps already, since we've all read this article. Let's look at these resource maps a little more closely now.*

Model the process of reading the resource maps on page 9 in *Indonesia's Rain Forests*. Focus on the title, labels, scale,.and key.

Discuss how using resource maps like these can help students learn new information and locate resources that can be found in a specific area. Ask questions such as:

What is one big idea you can learn from the resource maps in your books?

Have at least one student reading each of the books suggest answers.

Next, have students turn back to pages 18 and 19 in their books. Reread the three steps in the box at the bottom of page 18. As you read each step to the class, use the resource map on page 19 as a model. Continue to use examples from *Indonesia's Rain Forests*, but ask volunteers reading other books to offer similar information. For example:

1. Read the title.
Say: *The title tells me what the resource map shows. The title,* Main World Food Resources, *means this resource map shows where food resources are found around the world.*

2. Read the key.
Say: *By reading the key, I can see how to identify the symbols on the map. I can see that the symbol for rice is a triangle that points down.*

3. Study the map.
Say: *By studying the map, I can figure out where different food resources are grown. For example, I can see that rice is grown in the southern United States.*

Next, read the text at the bottom of page 19. Give students five minutes to write ideas they have about the map. Then have a brief class discussion about students' ideas related to the map.

Whole Class
- Introduce Genre Study

Small Groups
- Begin Reading: Pages 21–26

Whole Class
- Check Understanding

Introduce Genre Study

Whole Class

Problem-Solution Article

Explain to students that authors have varied purposes for writing. Authors can choose the writing form that best suits the purpose for writing. These different forms of writing are called genres. Say:

Writers use different forms, or genres, depending on their purpose for writing. Today we are going to learn about a genre, or type of writing, called a problem-solution article. Problem-solution articles describe a problem and give possible solutions to the problem.

Then have students turn to page 20 of their books. Read page 20 to the class. Say:

Look at this chart. It shows the important parts of a problem-solution article: the introduction, problem, and solution. Each part serves a different purpose. For example, the introduction outlines the problem discussed in the article.

Discuss the other parts of a problem-solution article with the class.

Next, have students turn to page 21. Explain to students that they will be reading a problem-solution article about the threat to the resources they read about in the informational article.

Then read and discuss the different labels shown on page 21, which identify and describe some parts of a problem-solution article.

Remind students that this problem-solution article is organized with the title, introduction, body paragraphs with the problem and solution information, photographs, and captions.

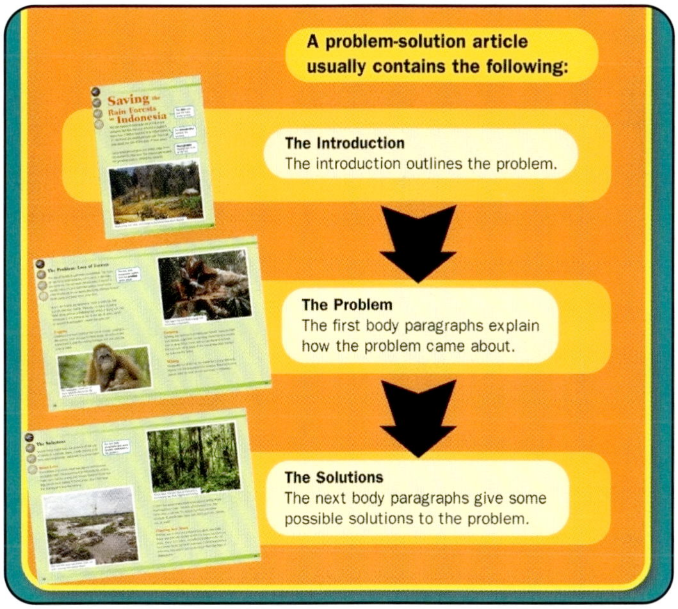

Begin Reading: Pages 21–26

Small Groups

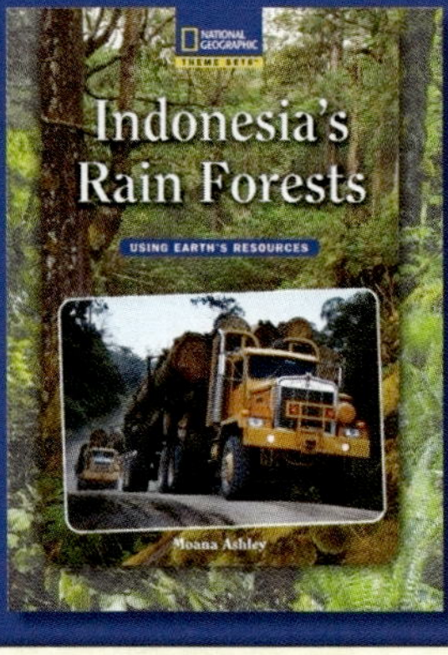

First Activity Block

With the Teacher

Begin Reading

- Review the genre.
- Model using the genre article.
- Read parts of the genre article.

Pairs

Fluency Practice

Students reading *Greenland's Ocean Region* pair up with students reading *Peru's Mountains*. Students reread aloud parts of Article 1 from their own books to practice reading fluency. To each pair, distribute the *Fluency Practice* Master on page 70 of this Teacher's Guide.

Individuals

Independent Reading

Students read *Saving the Environment in Australia*, Student Book pages 21–26.

To each student, distribute the *Content Reading Guide* Master, page 71 in this Teacher's Guide. Students should use the Master to take notes as they read for specific information.

Pairs

Fluency Practice

Students reading *Peru's Mountains* pair up with students reading *Greenland's Ocean Region*. Students reread aloud parts of Article 1 from their own books to practice reading fluency. To each pair, distribute the *Fluency Practice* Master on page 70 of this Teacher's Guide.

Second Activity Block

Pairs

Fluency Practice

Students reading *Indonesia's Rain Forests* pair up with students reading *Australia's Deserts*. Students reread aloud parts of Article 1 from their own books to practice reading fluency. To each pair, distribute the *Fluency Practice* Master on page 70 of this Teacher's Guide.

With the Teacher

Begin Reading

- Review the genre.
- Model using the genre article.
- Read parts of the genre article.

Pairs

Fluency Practice

Students reading *Australia's Deserts* pair up with students reading *Indonesia's Rain Forests*. Students reread aloud parts of Article 1 from their own books to practice reading fluency. To each pair, distribute the *Fluency Practice* Master on page 70 of this Teacher's Guide.

Individuals

Independent Reading

Students read *Saving the Mountains in Peru*, Student Book pages 21–26.

To each student, distribute the *Content Reading Guide* Master, page 71 in this Teacher's Guide. Students should use the Master to take notes as they read for specific information.

With the Teacher | Small Groups | ELL

Lesson Notes for *Indonesia's Rain Forest*

Model reading a problem-solution article

Have students turn to page 21 in their books. Ask them when they would read a problem-solution article. Discuss the parts of a problem-solution article. Have students flip through the article, noticing photographs, captions, and subheadings. Say:

We've just learned about Indonesia's rain forests. Now I'm going to read about what can be done to save the rain forests.

Model reading the first page of the problem-solution article, using the labels to point out information contained in it. Say:

We are going to take turns reading a problem-solution article. The first time we read, we will read to become familiar with the topic.

Reread the first page. Skim the text to point out three to five words that may be unfamiliar to the reader. Pronounce these words and discuss their meanings. Then have students read chorally or take turns reading. After students have finished reading, say:

We've just read a problem-solution article about Indonesia's rain forests. Now let's use the Key Concept statements to guide our reading.

Remind students of the Key Concepts by asking volunteers to name them.

Model reading for specific information

Distribute the *Content Reading Guide* Master, which students can use to guide them as they reread the problem-solution article. Model using the Key Concepts to show how you can read for specific information. Say:

The introduction tells me some trees are cut down for wood. This relates to Key Concept 2, that resources are useful to people in different ways.

Continue making connections between the text and Key Concept statements. Help students draw conclusions about content, such as how rain forest resources need to be conserved.

With the Teacher | Small Groups | ELL

Lesson Notes for *Greenland's Ocean Region*

Model reading a problem-solution article

Have students turn to page 21 in their books. Ask them when they would read a problem-solution article. Discuss the parts of a problem-solution article. Have students flip through the article, noticing photographs, captions, and subheadings. Say:

We've just learned about Greenland's ocean region. Now I'm going to read about what can be done to save the oceans.

Model reading the first page of the problem-solution article, using the labels to point out information contained in it. Say:

We are going to take turns reading a problem-solution article. The first time we read, we will read to become familiar with the topic.

Reread the first page. Skim the text to point out three to five words that may be unfamiliar to the reader. Pronounce these words and discuss their meanings. Then have students read chorally or take turns reading. After students have finished reading, say:

We've just read a problem-solution article about Greenland's ocean region. Now let's use the Key Concept statements to guide our reading.

Remind students of the Key Concepts by asking volunteers to name them.

Model reading for specific information

Distribute the *Content Reading Guide* Master, which students can use to guide them as they reread the problem-solution article. Model using the Key Concepts to show how you can read for specific information. Say:

The introduction tells me that the oceans are affected by pollution. This relates to Key Concept 3, that resources need to be conserved.

Continue making connections between the text and Key Concept statements. Help students draw conclusions about content, such as how ocean resources need to be protected.

Check Understanding

Whole Class

Discuss the Genre

Talk with students about how different types of writing, or genres, have different purposes. Ask:

What is the main reason you would use a problem-solution article? (to learn about how a problem came about and some possible solutions to the problem)

Then review the parts of a problem-solution article. Ask questions such as:

What are the parts of a problem-solution article?

What does the introduction tell you?

How are the body paragraphs organized?

Ask volunteers to share one problem they learned from the problem-solution article they read and to name a solution for that problem.

Share Learning

Have small groups of students share their books. Organize students into groups of four, with each student reading a different book.

Have each student walk through the problem-solution articles with group members, pointing out the title, introduction, subheadings, photographs, and captions.

Then each student should explain, in his or her own words, a problem and a solution from the article he or she read.

Read for Specific Information

Bring the class together to create a class chart, using information from the problem-solution articles and students' *Content Reading Guides*. Students can suggest information found in their own books or from a classmate's book. Use at least one example from each problem-solution article to show how the information in the problem-solution article relates to the Key Concepts.

After completing the chart, ask questions about the genre, such as:

When reading the problem-solution articles, was it easy to find information related to the Key Concepts?

Compare the problem-solution article to the first article in your book. How are these articles the same and how are they different? For example, how is each one organized?

Content Reading Guide		
Area and resource	**Information**	**Related Key Concept**
Indonesia/rain forests	Wood from rain forests is used to make furniture.	Key Concept 2
Greenland/ocean	The waters around Greenland are home to many different fish and other marine animals.	Key Concept 1
Australia/deserts	People mine for gold and copper in the Queen River Valley.	Key Concept 1
Peru/mountains	National parks can be created to protect threatened mountain areas.	Key Concept 3

Partially completed class chart

Lesson 5

Whole Class
• Introduce Key Concept Activities

Small Groups
• Finish Reading: Pages 21–26

Whole Class
• Check Understanding

Introduce Key Concept Activities

Whole Class ELL

Have students turn to page 27 in their books. Read the title of the page and point out that there is one activity for each Key Concept statement.

Summarize each activity, and make sure students understand what the product of each activity should be (a list, a chart, or a letter). Use the art next to each activity to aid in the discussion. Remind students that they can use information from the informational and genre articles to complete each activity.

Assigning the Activities

During Lesson 5, students can work in pairs or small groups as they begin working on the Key Concept Activities. Students can complete as much as they can during this Lesson, but they should be able to complete at least one activity.

Activity summaries

Key Concept Activity 1
This activity asks students to make a list of things they use each day that come from natural resources.

Key Concept Activity 2
This activity asks students to make a chart of the properties and uses of natural resources.

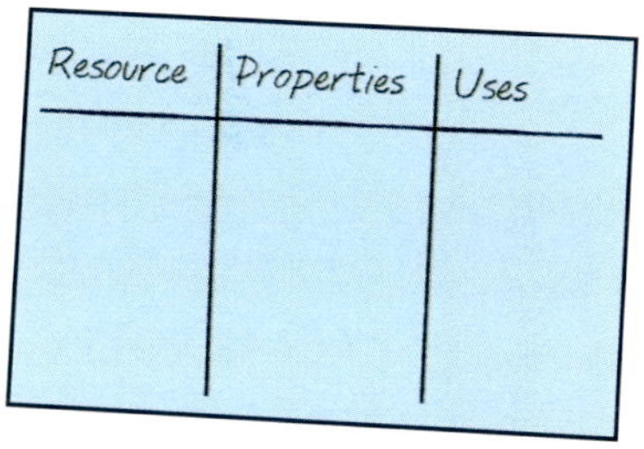

Key Concept Activity 3
This activity asks students to write a letter to a conservation group.

Lesson 5

Finish Reading: Pages 21–26

Small Groups

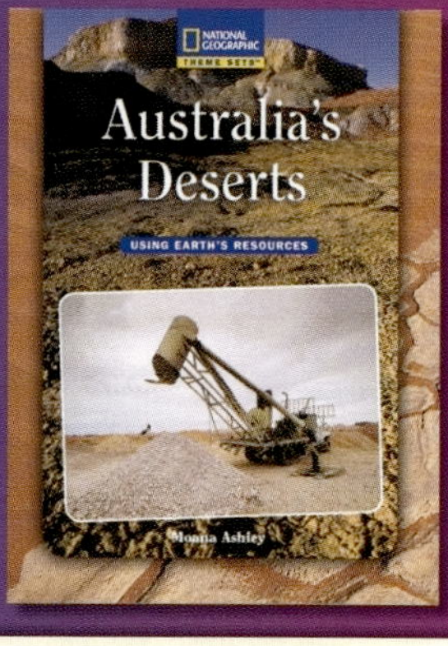

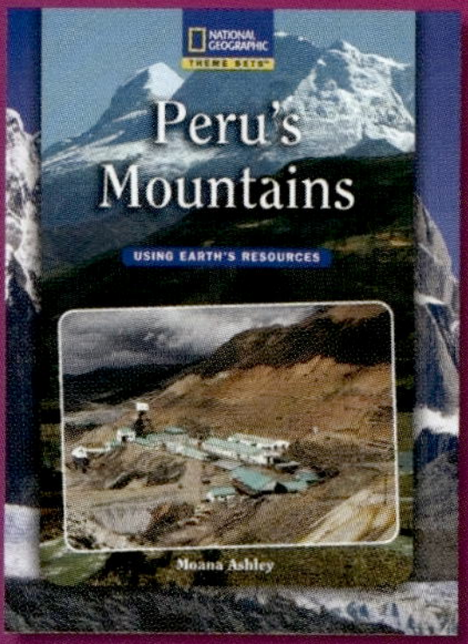

First Activity Block

Pairs/Groups

Key Concept Activities

Students can work in pairs or small groups to complete Key Concept Activity 1. They can also begin Key Concept Activity 2 at this time.

Students should use the Student Book to complete these activities.

Pairs/Groups

Key Concept Activities

Students can work in pairs or small groups to complete Key Concept Activity 1. They can also begin Key Concept Activity 2 at this time.

Students should use the Student Book to complete these activities.

With the Teacher

Discuss and Reread

- Review the genre.
- Review using the genre article.
- Reread parts of the genre article.

Pairs/Groups

Key Concept Activities

Students can work in pairs or small groups to complete Key Concept Activity 1. They can also begin Key Concept Activities 2 and 3 at this time.

Students should use the Student Book to complete these activities.

Second Activity Block

Pairs/Groups

Continue Key Concept Activities

Students can continue working on Key Concept Activities 2 and 3. Time permitting, the teacher can meet with students reading *Indonesia's Rain Forests* to assess students' progress on the Key Concept activities.

Pairs/Groups

Continue Key Concept Activities

Students can continue working on Key Concept Activities 2 and 3. Time permitting, the teacher can meet with students reading *Greenland's Ocean Region* to assess students' progress on the Key Concept activities.

Pairs/Groups

Key Concept Activities

Students can work in pairs or small groups to complete Key Concept Activity 1. They can also begin Key Concept Activities 2 and 3 at this time.

Students should use the Student Book to complete these activities.

With the Teacher

Discuss and Reread

- Review the genre.
- Review using the genre article.
- Reread parts of the genre article.

With the Teacher | Small Groups | ELL

Lesson Notes for *Australia's Deserts*

Review reading a problem-solution article

Have students bring their *Content Reading Guide* Masters to the discussion. Have them turn to page 21 in their books.

Have students flip through the problem-solution article. Point out the photographs, captions, and subheadings. Model reading the first page of the problem-solution article, using the labels to point out information contained in it. Say:

We are going to take turns rereading Saving the Environment in Australia. *As we read, we will become more familiar with the topic.*

Have students take turns rereading the problem-solution article. As needed, stop and explain any words or concepts students may need help understanding. After students have finished reading, say:

We've just read a problem-solution article about Australia's environment. Now let's review the Key Concept statements that guided our reading.

Remind students of the Key Concepts by asking volunteers to name them.

Review reading for specific information

Say:

You used the Key Concepts to reread the article for specific information to learn more about the topic. Look at your Content Reading Guides and let's discuss what you found.

Then call on volunteers to name one of their links between specific information and a Key Concept. Correct any misconceptions. Continue until students have all contributed. If students have not finished finding specific information for the Key Concepts, finish as a group or direct them to go to their seats to finish.

With the Teacher | Small Groups | ELL

Lesson Notes for *Peru's Mountains*

Review reading a problem-solution article

Have students bring their *Content Reading Guide* Masters to the discussion. Have them turn to page 21 in their books.

Have students flip through the problem-solution article. Point out the photographs, captions, and subheadings. Model reading the first page of the problem-solution article, using the labels to point out information contained in it. Say:

We are going to take turns rereading Saving the Mountains in Peru. *As we read, we will become more familiar with the topic.*

Have students take turns rereading the problem-solution article. As needed, stop and explain any words or concepts students may need help understanding. After students have finished reading, say:

We've just read a problem-solution article about Peru's mountains. Now let's review the Key Concept statements that guided our reading.

Remind students of the Key Concepts by asking volunteers to name them.

Review reading for specific information

Say:

You used the Key Concepts to reread the article for specific information to learn more about the topic. Look at your Content Reading Guides and let's discuss what you found.

Then call on volunteers to name one of their links between specific information and a Key Concept. Correct any misconceptions. Continue until students have all contributed. If students have not finished finding specific information for the Key Concepts, finish as a group or direct them to go to their seats to finish.

Check Understanding

Whole Class

Share Learning

By now, all students have read the first article and the genre article in the Student Book. They have worked together in mixed groups, in pairs, and as a class to discuss the Key Concepts. They have worked independently on the Key Concept Activities found on page 27 of the Student Book.

Now students can come together in mixed groups to share the Key Concept Activities they have completed. Organize students into groups of four, with each student reading a different book. Explain that each student should share his or her work on the Key Concept Activities and compare how other members of the group completed the same assignment. Students should be able to explain another group member's activity, compared to his or her own.

Students can use questions like these to guide their discussion:

How is this group member's information similar to the information I've found?

How is this information different?

How does this information relate to the Key Concepts?

After groups of students have finished discussing their projects, bring the class together. Students can share what they've learned by comparing a group member's project with their own.

Use the questions shown above as a guide for the class discussion.

Assessment Check

Key Concept Activity 1

Lists should

- ✔ include four items used everyday.
- ✔ include the natural resource each item comes from.
- ✔ be neatly completed.

Key Concept Activity 2

Charts should

- ✔ have column headings.
- ✔ list at least three natural resources found in the area.
- ✔ include the properties for each resource and the ways each is used.

Key Concept Activity 3

Letters should

- ✔ be written in a letter format.
- ✔ list two reasons a resource should be conserved.
- ✔ offer a suggestion for conservation.
- ✔ be neatly completed.

RESEARCH AND WRITE

Introduce Research and Write

Explain that students will write their own problem-solution articles.

Have students turn to the Research and Write activity beginning on page 28 in their books. Explain that students will be working on steps 1–3 today and steps 4 and 5 in the next writing lesson. Then say:

I am going to read the introduction from the Indonesia's Rain Forests *book. This introduction is specific to this book, but the introductions in your books will refer to the book you read. Follow along silently as I read to the class.*

Read the introduction and allow time for students to ask questions.

1. Study the Model ELL

Read step 1 to the class. Then have students turn to page 21. Say:

On this page, you will find the beginning of a problem-solution article. We are going to use the problem-solution article on pages 21–26 as a model for writing our own problem-solution articles.

Look at the title. Notice how the title is in large letters and easy to read. Titles should stand out from the rest of the information. The problem-solution articles you write should have a title that is easy to read.

Continue in this way with each of the important parts of the problem-solution articles. Then read the text in the blue box on page 28. This box lists the important parts of writing a problem-solution article.

2. Choose Your Topic

Read step 2 to the class. Remind students that they should choose just one conservation issue to write a problem-solution article about. They can look in the library or on the Internet to get ideas for their problem-solution articles.

3. Research Your Topic

Read step 3 to the class. Distribute the *Prewriting* Master to students. Explain that they will use this Master to organize their research and take notes. Read the introduction on the Master and discuss each part.

Students can work in pairs or independently to review the model and conduct research. Students can ask a classmate to help answer questions they may have. As students conduct research, circulate around the classroom to check that students are using the *Prewriting* Master correctly.

Check Progress

Bring the class together to discuss students' progress. Ask questions such as:

Has everyone chosen a topic and completed his or her research?

Are you finding enough information about your topic?

Remind students that they will have time to write, revise, and edit. They will then create a poster about their conservation issue to present to the class.

Writing a Problem-Solution Article

- Choose a topic related to conservation. The topic must have a problem and possible solutions.
- Write an introduction explaining what needs to be conserved.
- Write several body paragraphs describing the problem.
- Write several more paragraphs giving some solutions to the problem.

RESEARCH AND WRITE

Discuss the Writing

Whole Class

Briefly discuss students' progress. Review pages 28–29 in the Student Book.

4. Write a Draft

Read step 4 to the class while students follow along silently. Remind students that when writing a draft, they should focus on getting their ideas on paper. They can fix spelling and grammar mistakes as they review and edit. Circulate around the room and meet with students to help them work through questions they may have about their writing.

5. Revise Your Draft

Read step 5 to the class. Remind students that they can also use a peer editor during this step. Peer editors should focus on spelling, grammar, punctuation, sense, and interest level.

Assessment Check

A well-written problem-solution article

- ✔ Ideas are clear and focused.
- ✔ The introduction states the problem clearly.
- ✔ The problem and solution paragraphs give information that is interesting and important.
- ✔ Information is organized according to the problem-solution article in the Student Book.
- ✔ Writing is free of mechanical errors.

An average problem-solution article

- ✔ Ideas are fairly clear.
- ✔ The introduction states the problem somewhat clearly.
- ✔ The problem and solution paragraphs give information that is somewhat interesting and important.
- ✔ Information is organized according to some parts of the problem-solution article in the Student Book.
- ✔ Writing has some mechanical errors.

A poorly-written problem-solution article

- ✔ Ideas are unfocused.
- ✔ The introduction does not state the problem clearly.
- ✔ The problem and solution paragraphs give information that is not interesting or important.
- ✔ Information is not organized according to the problem-solution article in the Student Book.
- ✔ Writing has many mechanical errors.

SHARING YOUR WORK

Create A Conservation Poster

Small Groups

As a class, have students turn to page 30 in their books. Read page 30 aloud to the class as students follow along silently. Explain that students will work independently to make a poster about their conservation issues.

Review the following steps with the class so that students understand each step in the process. Each student should participate in all the steps.

Individual Work

Step 1. Think of a slogan. Write a catchy phrase on your poster to draw people's attention.

Step 2. Include a strong photograph or illustration. Find a photograph of the animal or environment you want to conserve. Put the photograph on your poster.

Step 3. Write some information about the cause. Write a paragraph about the important issues related to your topic. Be sure to include important facts. Include this information on your poster.

Share Your Conservation Posters

When each student has completed each of these three steps, have students display their posters at the front of the class. Give students time to review the display over the next few days and ask each other questions about each other's posters. Students can work independently or in pairs to answer the following questions in their notebooks:

What did you like most about creating a conservation poster?

Did you learn something new from someone else's conservation poster?

After a few days, bring the class together to discuss the display. Ask volunteers to respond to what they found interesting.

Masters	Purpose
Prereading: Word Web	Provides a tool for recording students' prior knowledge about the topic before they read
Indonesia's Rain Forests Vocabulary **Greenland's Ocean Region Vocabulary** **Australia's Deserts Vocabulary** **Peru's Mountains Vocabulary**	Provides a tool for developing strategies for book-level vocabulary
Comprehension Model	Provides a Master that can be made into a transparency to model the comprehension strategy
Comprehension Strategy	Provides a tool to help students practice the comprehension strategy
Word Cards, Indonesia's Rain Forests **Word Cards, Greenland's Ocean Region**	Provides cards that can be cut out and used to develop vocabulary
Share Learning	Provides a tool students can use in small groups to compare content across all Student Books
Key Concept Questions	Provides a tool students can use in small groups to answer the Key Concept questions shown on page 17 in the Student Book
Fluency Practice	Provides a tool for pairs of students as they reread the text to improve fluency
Content Reading Guide	Provides a tool to help students record specific information
Prewriting	Provides a tool for organizing students' ideas before they write
Open-Book Test	Provides an opportunity for students to demonstrate both their understanding of the content and their ability to read for specific information
Indonesia's Rain Forests Test **Greenland's Ocean Region Test** **Australia's Deserts Test** **Peru's Mountains Test**	Provides an opportunity for students to demonstrate their understanding of the content with differentiated multiple-choice and short-answer questions

Name ______________________ Book title ______________________

Prereading: Word Web

You will be reading about Earth's resources. In the ovals of the web, write the natural resources you know. On the lines by each oval, write the ways that the natural resource is used. After reading Article 1, add more information to your web. You can add as many ovals and lines as you need.

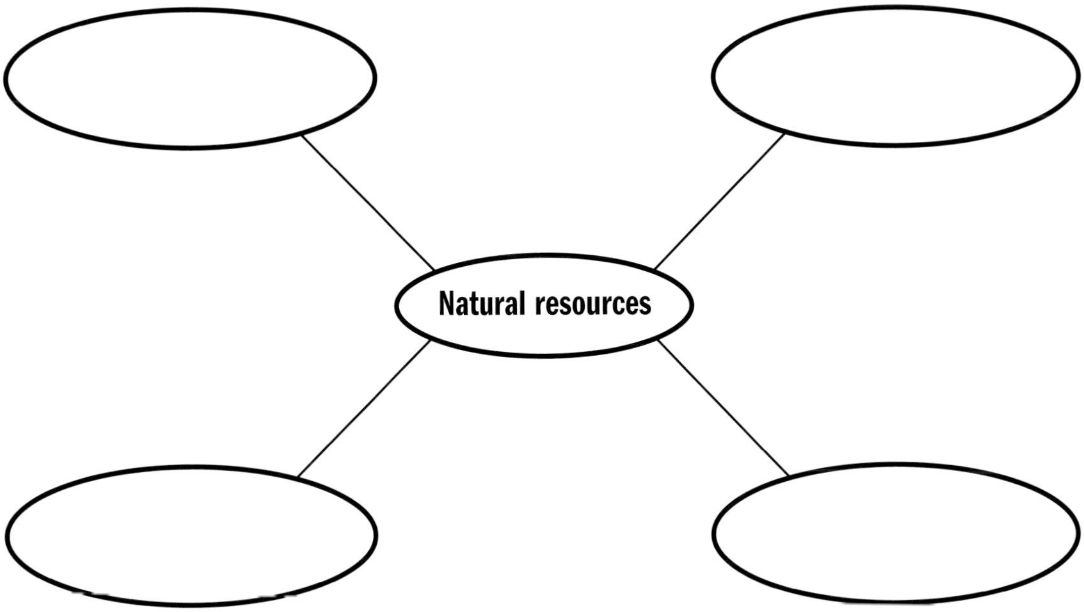

Name ______________________________

Vocabulary: Word Knowledge Chart

The words below are from *Indonesia's Rain Forests*. Put a check mark in the box that describes how well you know the word. If you know the word, write the definition. If you do not know the word, look it up in the glossary and then write the definition in the last column.

Word	Know the word well	Have heard the word	Know nothing about the word	Definition
1. conservation				
2. natural resources				
3. recycling				
4. climate				
5. malaria				
6. properties				
7. renewable				

Name ________________________________

Vocabulary: Word Knowledge Chart

The words below are from *Greenland's Ocean Region*. Put a check mark in the box that describes how well you know the word. If you know the word, write the definition. If you do not know the word, look it up in the glossary and then write the definition in the last column.

Word	Know the word well	Have heard the word	Know nothing about the word	Definition
1. conservation				
2. natural resources				
3. recycling				
4. marine				
5. nutrients				
6. protein				
7. renewable				

Name ____________________________________

Vocabulary: Word Knowledge Chart

The words below are from *Australia's Deserts*. Put a check mark in the box that describes how well you know the word. If you know the word, write the definition. If you do not know the word, look it up in the glossary and then write the definition in the last column.

Word	Know the word well	Have heard the word	Know nothing about the word	Definition
1. conservation				
2. natural resources				
3. recycling				
4. coal				
5. exports				
6. minerals				
7. mining				

Name ______________________

Vocabulary: Word Knowledge Chart

The words below are from *Peru's Mountains*. Put a check mark in the box that describes how well you know the word. If you know the word, write the definition. If you do not know the word, look it up in the glossary and then write the definition in the last column.

Word	Know the word well	Have heard the word	Know nothing about the word	Definition
1. conservation				
2. natural resources				
3. recycling				
4. altitudes				
5. deforestation				
6. minerals				
7. replenished				

Name ______________________ Book title ______________________

Comprehension Model: Making Inferences

Handle with Care

Save energy! Don't litter! Reduce air pollution! Do these environmental slogans make a difference in protecting the environment? The answer is yes. Even the efforts of one person can help protect our planet.

Plants and animals, including humans, need food and water to survive. These needs are met by the **natural resources** found on Earth. We grow much of our food in the soil of Earth. If soil can be blown or washed away by wind and water, the soil gets damaged and rich farmland can be turned into a desert wasteland. Farmers plant trees and use better farming practices to prevent this from happening.

Trees are also important for the air we breathe. Trees use carbon dioxide and make the oxygen we need to live. Also, when trees are cut down, many plants and animals lose their habitat. The **conservation** of trees is important to protecting the environment.

The average American produces 10 tons of trash in 13 years. This trash ends up in landfills that pollute the water, air, and land. We can also help to protect the environment by **recycling**, reusing, and reducing what we throw away. In fact, about 80 percent of household trash can be recycled. If everyone worked harder to recycle, we could protect the environment.

The trash we produce pollutes water, air, and land.

Steps for Making Inferences

- Ask questions about what you read.
- Study the pictures to get clues about what you are reading.
- Use words, visuals, and what you already know to make inferences.

Name ______________________ Book title ______________________

Comprehension Strategy: Making Inferences

Use this chart as you read. Write facts and details from what you read in column 1. Write what you already know in column 2. Then write what you can infer in column 3.

What I read	What I know	What I can infer

Name ____________________

Word Cards: Indonesia's Rain Forests

Cut along the dotted lines. Work with a partner to put the words in categories such as "environment." Some words may be in more than one category.

climate	the general weather conditions of a certain area
conservation	protection and careful use of natural resources
malaria	a tropical disease that causes severe fever and sometimes death
natural resources	materials that are found in nature and are useful to people
nonrenewable	not able to be replaced once it is used
properties	special features or qualities
recycling	turning used material into new products
renewable	able to be replaced by nature once it is used

Name ______________________________

Word Cards: Greenland's Ocean Region

Cut along the dotted lines. Work with a partner to put the words in categories such as "environment." Some words may be in more than one category.

conservation	protection and careful use of natural resources
marine	relating to the ocean
natural resources	materials that are found in nature and are useful to people
nonrenewable	not able to be replaced once it is used
nutrients	substances that help people or animals grow or remain healthy
properties	special features or qualities
recycling	turning used material into new products
renewable	able to be replaced by nature once it is used

Name ______________________ Book title ______________________

Share Learning

Work with students who have read books different from yours. Each group member is the expert on one area where natural resources are found. Each member should share information from his or her book to complete a row on the chart.

Resource location	Resources from the area	How resources are used	How resources can be conserved

Name ______________________ Book title ______________________

Key Concept Questions

Read the questions on page 17 of your book. Think about what you have learned from reading your book. Then answer the questions below.

1. Name two or more resources from the country you read about in this book.
2. Name at least three ways the natural resources discussed in this book are used.
3. Explain the difference between a renewable resource and a nonrenewable resource.
4. Give at least two examples of how people can conserve Earth's resources.

Name ______________________ **Book title** ______________________

Fluency Practice

You will be reading parts of your book with a partner. You will take turns being the reader and the listener.

Readers will read from their own books. You will pick a short section to read, and you will read this same section three times.

Listeners will correct missed words. When you hear a missed word, say, STOP, and the word. Have the reader repeat this word. Then ask the reader to read that sentence again. Tell the reader how to improve after each reading, and then fill out the checklist for the reader.

Reading Checklist

Reader Name: ______________________

Reading #1:	great	good	so-so	not very good
Reading #2:	great	good	so-so	not very good
Reading #3:	great	good	so-so	not very good

Check how the reader improved

_____ My partner read more smoothly.

_____ My partner knew more words.

_____ My partner stopped for more punctuation.

_____ My partner read with more expression.

Name ______________________ Book title ______________________

Content Reading Guide: Problem-Solution Article

You can read a problem-solution article to find out about a problem and some possible solutions to the problem. As you read pages 21–26 in your book, look for information related to the Key Concept statements. Then write information you find in the problem-solution article that relates to the Key Concepts and tell which Key Concept it relates to.

Topic: ______________________

Information	Related Key Concept

Name ______________________ Book title ______________________

Prewriting

You will be writing a problem-solution article. Your article should include information about a conservation issue that you think people need to know about. Use the problem-solution article beginning on page 21 as a model.

Issue: ______________________

Main problem: ______________________

____

____

Reasons for this problem: ______________________

____

____

____

Possible solutions to this problem: ______________________

____

____

____

Other important information: ______________________

____

____

____

____

Name ______________________ Book title ______________________

Open-Book Test

1. ______________ are materials that are found in nature and are useful to people.
2. Turning used material into new products is called ______________.
3. ______________ is the protection and careful use of natural resources.
4. What are some of the natural resources that are found in the area you read about and how are they used? ______________
5. What is the difference between a renewable resource and a nonrenewable resource?
6. What are some renewable resources found in the area you read about?
7. What are some nonrenewable resources found in the area you read about?
8. What can be done to protect the natural resources in the area you read about?
9. Look at the problem-solution article starting on page 21. What is the problem discussed in this article? What are the causes of this problem?
10. What are some possible solutions to this problem?

INDONESIA'S RAIN FORESTS

Name ______________________________

Test

Circle the letter of the correct answer.

1. Tropical rain forests

A. are warm in summer and cold in winter.

B. are not a good source of hardwood.

C. grow new trees as fast as they are used up.

D. provide much of Earth's oxygen.

2. All of the following are made from rain forest resources EXCEPT

A. paper.

B. gemstones.

C. cooking oil.

D. medicine.

3. Rain forest trees are examples of

A. nonrenewable resources.

B. properties.

C. natural resources.

D. all of the above.

4. Recycling is defined as

A. turning used material into new products.

B. a material that is used and then replaced by nature.

C. protection and careful use of natural resources.

D. materials that are found in nature and are useful to people.

5. A problem-solution article

A. tries to convince the reader which solution to use.

B. presents several possible solutions to a problem.

C. tells the right solution to use.

D. explains why there are no solutions to a problem.

---

6. Explain why Indonesia's rain forests need to be conserved and two ways people can help conserve them.

____

____

____

Use the map to answer questions 7–8.

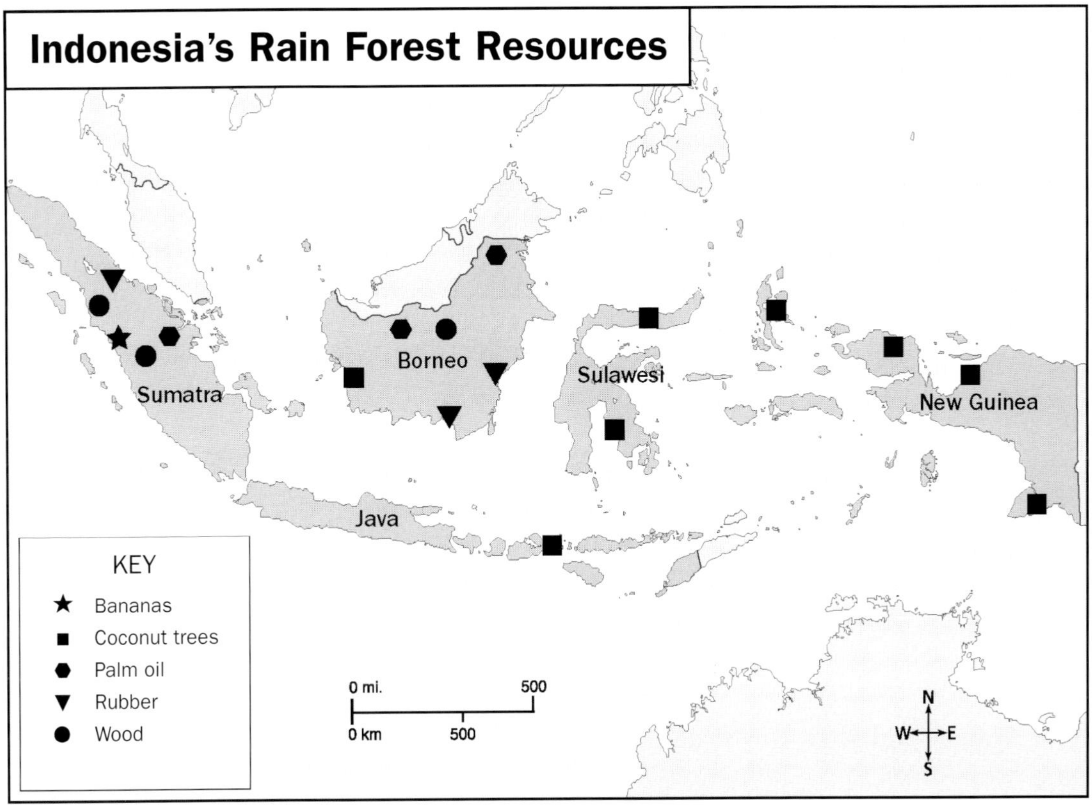

7. Write a sentence that tells what this map shows.

____

____

____

8. What resource is found most commonly in Indonesia according to this map? How do you know?

____

____

____

GREENLAND'S OCEAN REGION

Name ______________________________

Test

Circle the letter of the correct answer.

1. The oceans around Greenland are

A. full of nutrients.

B. important in the water cycle.

C. home to many marine animals.

D. all of the above.

2. All of the following are made from ocean resources EXCEPT

A. fertilizer.

B. coal.

C. pet food.

D. rain water.

3. Halibut and salmon are examples of

A. nonrenewable resources.

B. properties.

C. natural resources.

D. all of the above.

4. Recycling is defined as

A. turning used materials into new products.

B. a material that is used and then replaced by nature.

C. protection and careful use of natural resources.

D. materials that are found in nature and are useful to people.

5. A problem-solution article

A. tries to convince the reader which solution to use.

B. presents several possible solutions to a problem.

C. tells the right solution to use.

D. explains why there are no solutions to a problem.

---

6. Explain why the oceans around Greenland need to be protected and two ways that we can conserve these resources.

____

____

____

GREENLAND'S OCEAN REGION

Use the map to answer questions 7–8.

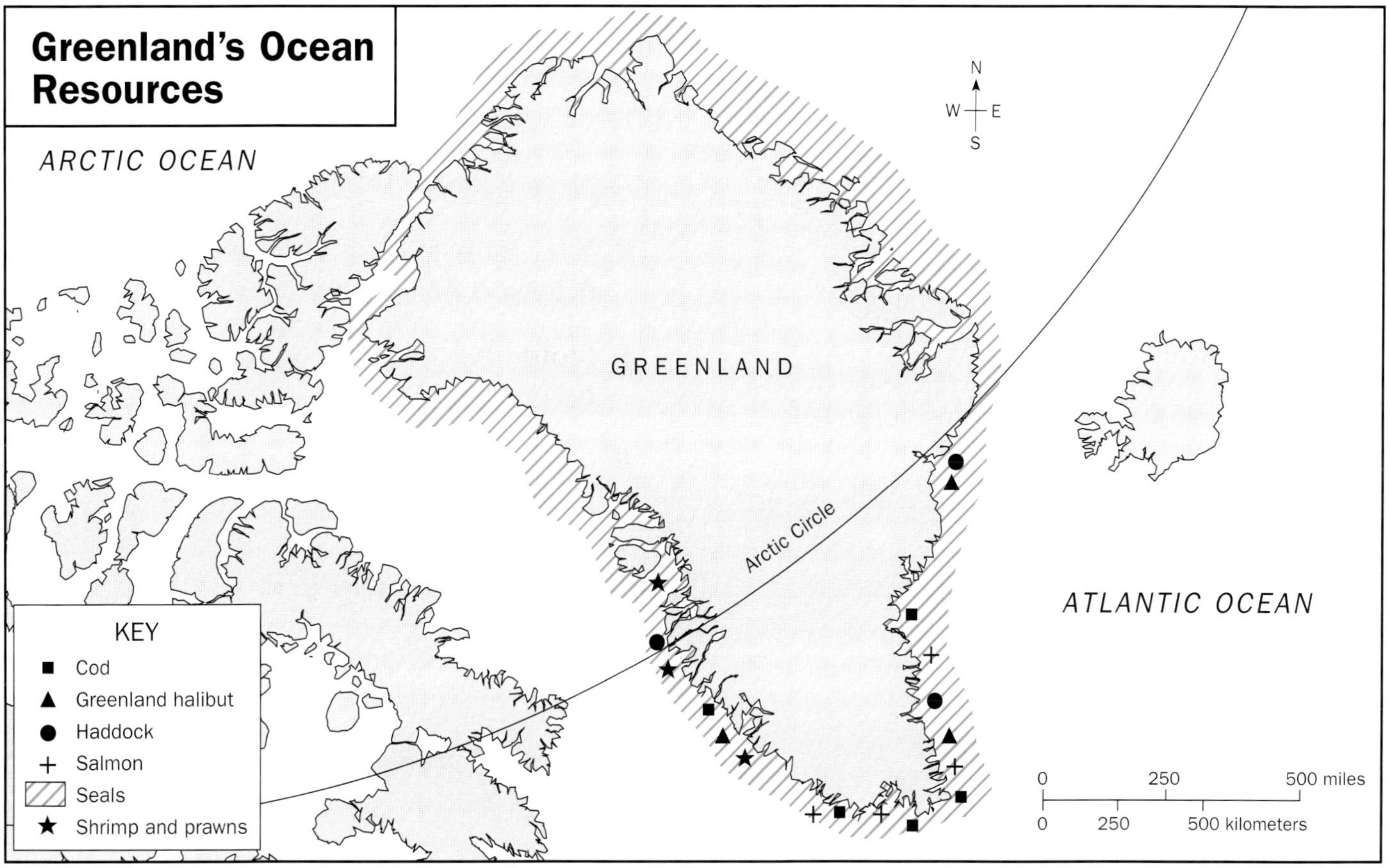

7. Write a sentence that tells what this map shows.

____

____

____

8. What resource is found all around Greenland? How do you know?

____

____

____

AUSTRALIA'S DESERTS

Name ______________________

Test

Circle the letter of the correct answer.

1. Australia's deserts have
   - A. few natural resources.
   - B. many plant resources.
   - C. natural resources that are easy to replace.
   - D. many natural resources underground.

2. All of the following are made from desert resources EXCEPT
   - A. electricity.
   - B. clothing.
   - C. jewelry.
   - D. plumbing parts.

3. Copper is an example of
   - A. a renewable resource.
   - B. a fuel.
   - C. a natural resource.
   - D. all of the above.

4. Recycling is defined as
   - A. turning used materials into new products.
   - B. a material that is used and then replaced by nature.
   - C. protection and careful use of natural resources.
   - D. materials that are found in nature and are useful to people.

5. A problem-solution article
   - A. tries to convince the reader which solution to use.
   - B. presents several possible solutions to a problem.
   - C. tells the right solution to use.
   - D. explains why there are no solutions to a problem.

---

6. Explain why Australia's desert resources need to be conserved and two ways people can help conserve them.

____

____

____

Use the map to answer questions 7–8.

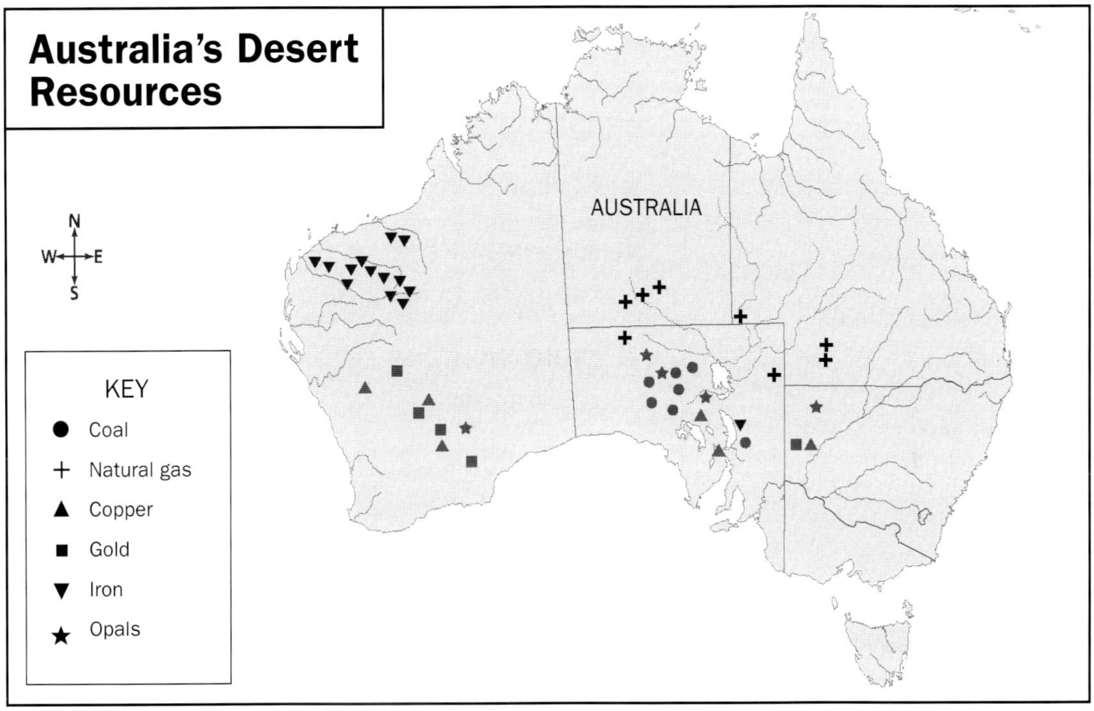

7. Write a sentence that tells what this map shows.

____

____

____

8. What do you know about iron mines from looking at this resource map?

____

____

____

PERU'S MOUNTAINS

Name ______________________

Test

Circle the letter of the correct answer.

1. The Andes mountains

A. provide Peru with a huge mining industry.

B. affect the climate of the region.

C. are in danger of being deforested.

D. all of the above.

2. All of the following are made from Peruvian Andes minerals EXCEPT

A. alloys.

B. quinine.

C. jewelry.

D. electrical wires.

3. Timber is an example of

A. a nonrenewable resource.

B. a mineral.

C. a natural resource.

D. all of the above.

4. Recycling is defined as

A. turning used materials into new products.

B. a material that is used and then replaced by nature.

C. protection and careful use of natural resources.

D. materials that are found in nature and are useful to people.

5. A problem-solution article

A. tries to convince the reader which solution to use.

B. presents several possible solutions to a problem.

C. tells the right solution to use.

D. explains why there are no solutions to a problem.

---

6. Explain why Peru's mountain resources need to be conserved and two ways people can help conserve them.

____

____

____

Use the map to answer questions 7–8.

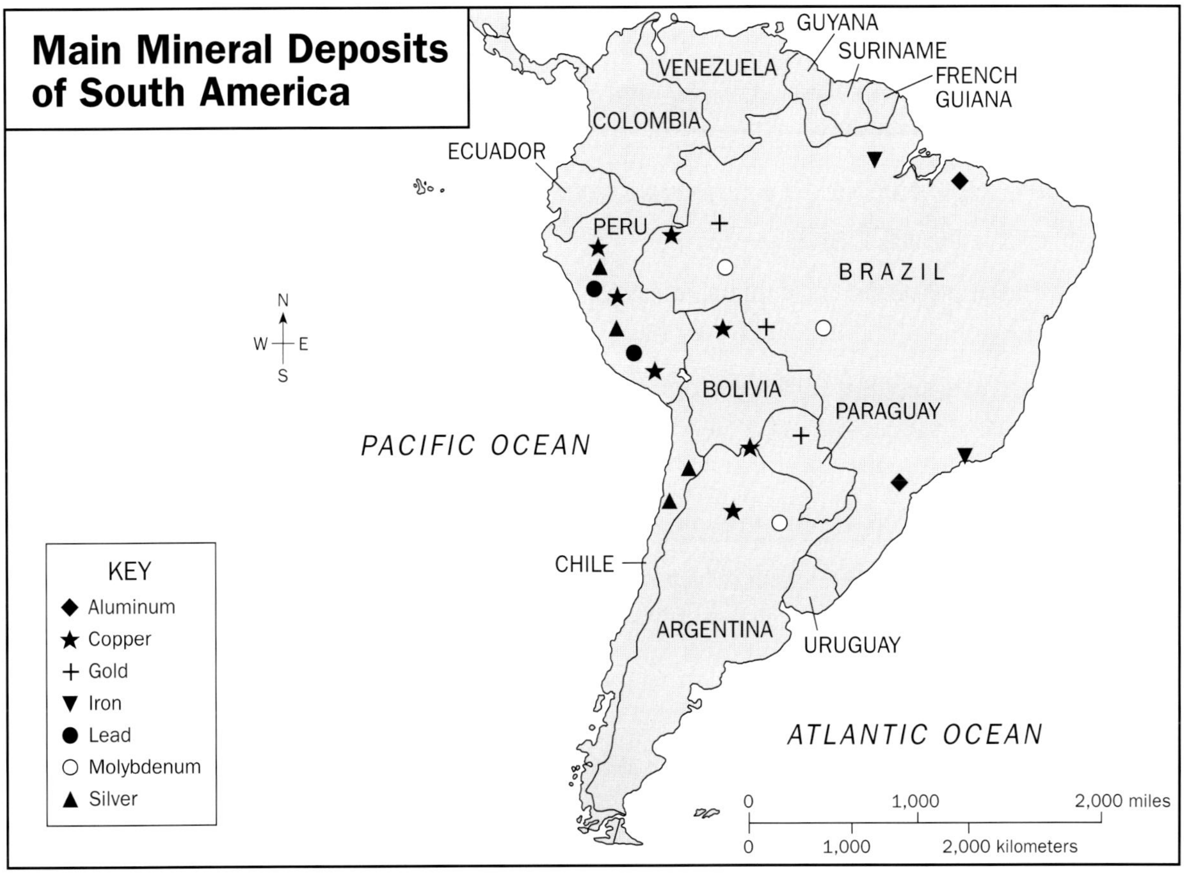

7. Write a sentence that tells what this map shows.

____

____

____

8. What do you know about copper from looking at this resource map?

____

____

____

Test Answers

OPEN-BOOK TEST

Distribute the *Open-Book Test* Master to students. This allows students to demonstrate both their understanding of the content and their ability to read for specific information. Students should work quietly and independently to complete this test during this 20-minute period.

Test Questions

1. [Natural resources] **are materials that are found in nature and are useful to people**
2. **Turning used material into new products is called** [recycling]**.**
3. [Conservation] **is the protection and careful use of natural resources.**

4. What are some of the natural resources that are found in the area you read about and how are they used?	trees—for fruits and nuts to eat and wood for building, making paper, and medicines
5. What is the difference between a renewable resource and a nonrenewable resource?	A renewable resource can be replaced by nature. A nonrenewable resource does not get replaced and can get used up.
6. What are some renewable resources found in the area you read about?	animals, plants, fresh water
7. What are some nonrenewable resources found in the area you read about?	metals, gemstones, oil, natural gas, coal
8. What can be done to protect the natural resources in the area you read about?	Protect the forests, use less paper, buy fewer wood items, and recycle.
9. Look at the problem-solution article starting on page 21. What is the problem discussed in this article? What are the causes of this problem?	The rain forests of Indonesia are being destroyed because of logging, farming, and mining.
10. What are some possible solutions to this problem?	Strict laws against cutting down trees, planting new trees, and conservation can help to solve the problem.

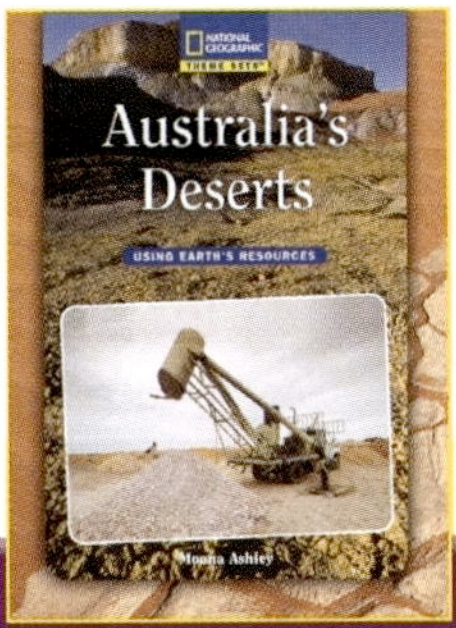

marine animals—for food, clothing, and fertilizer	minerals and metals—for building; gemstones—for making jewelry; fuels—to heat homes	trees—to get fruit for food; medicines, wood for building; metals—to make electrical wires and jewelry
A renewable resource can be replaced by nature. A nonrenewable resource does not get replaced and can get used up.	A renewable resource can be replaced by nature. A nonrenewable resource does not get replaced and can get used up.	A renewable resource can be replaced by nature. A nonrenewable resource does not get replaced and can get used up.
animals, plants, fresh water	animals, plants, fresh water	animals, plants, fresh water
metals, gemstones, oil, natural gas, coal	metals, gemstones, oil, natural gas, coal	metals, gemstones, oil, natural gas, coal
Limit fishing and seal hunting, and recycle water.	Use less electricity, use more efficient heating and cooling systems, and recycle.	Protect resource areas and recycle.
The ocean region around Greenland is being polluted by industrial chemicals, mining, and oil exploration.	The environment in Australia is being harmed because of water and air pollution.	The mountain forests are being destroyed by deforestation and pollution.
Reducing pollution, using safer mining methods, using an oil spill sensitivity atlas, and protecting certain areas can help to solve the problem.	Using safer mining methods, improving cleanup methods, and conservation can help to solve the problem.	Creating national parks, using better farming methods and safer mining methods, and conservation can help to solve the problem.

Answers to Multiple-Choice Questions

1. **D**
2. **B**
3. **C**
4. **A**
5. **B**

Scoring Guides

Struggling readers may provide responses that are less complete than those provided by more advanced readers. You can take this into account when grading students' responses.

Question 6

Complete The response explains why Indonesia's rain forests need to be conserved and two ways to conserve them. The need for conservation may include the importance of the rain forest for oxygen or in the oxygen cycle; the destruction, or cutting down, of the rain forest; the fact that rain forest trees are being cut down or used faster than Earth can replace them; erosion, or the washing away, of soil; or the loss or extinction of many types of plants and animals. Ways to conserve the rain forests may include passing laws that protect the rain forest, buying fewer products made from rain forest wood, recycling paper, or planting new trees.

Partial The response includes an explanation for why Indonesia's rain forest need to be conserved and only one way to do so or two ways to conserve the rain forests but no explanation for why.

Unsatisfactory/Incorrect The response includes little or no information related to conserving Indonesia's rain forests.

Question 7

Complete The response is a complete sentence that tells what the map mostly shows. The response includes information related to Indonesia's rain forest resources, such as what they are (bananas, coconut trees, palm oil, rubber, and wood) and where they are found.

Partial The response is a complete or incomplete sentence that tells what the map partly shows. The response includes some information related to Indonesia's rain forest resources but is not detailed.

Unsatisfactory/Incorrect The response is an incomplete sentence that does not relate to the map. The response does not refer to Indonesia's rain forest resources.

Question 8

Complete The response identifies coconut trees as the resource found most commonly in Indonesia and explains that its symbol appears more often than any other resource on the map.

Partial The response identifies coconut trees as the resource found most commonly in Indonesia.

Unsatisfactory/Incorrect The response does not identify coconut trees as the resource found most commonly in Indonesia.

Answers to Multiple-Choice Questions

1. **D**
2. **B**
3. **C**
4. **A**
5. **B**

Scoring Guides

Struggling readers may provide responses that are less complete than those provided by more advanced readers. You can take this into account when grading students' responses.

Question 6

Complete The response explains why Greenland's oceans need to be conserved and two ways to conserve them. The need for conservation may include the importance of the oceans in the water cycle, the need for clean water, the fact that some marine animals are endangered, the lower numbers of marine animals through hunting and fishing, or the harm that waste water and/or pollution do to sea animals. Ways to conserve the oceans' resources may include laws that protect marine animals, limits on how many fish boats can catch, recycling, collecting and cleaning waste water, reducing pollution, stopping the use of poisonous chemicals and pesticides, or using oil spill sensitivity atlases to reduce oil spill damage.

Partial The response includes an explanation for why Greenland's oceans need to be conserved and only one way to do so or two ways to conserve the oceans but no explanation for why.

Unsatisfactory/Incorrect The response includes little or no information related to conserving Greenland's oceans.

Question 7

Complete The response is a complete sentence that tells what the map mostly shows. The response includes information related to Greenland's ocean resources, such as what they are (cod, Greenland halibut, haddock, salmon, seals, and shrimp and prawns), and where they are found.

Partial The response is a complete or incomplete sentence that tells what the map partly shows. The response includes some information related to Greenland's ocean resources, but is not detailed.

Unsatisfactory/Incorrect The response is an incomplete sentence that does not relate to the map. The response does not refer to Greenland's ocean resources.

Question 8

Complete The response identifies seals as the resource found all around Greenland and explains that the symbol appears more often than any other resource on the map.

Partial The response identifies seals as the resource found all around Greenland.

Unsatisfactory/Incorrect The response does not identify seals as the resource found all around Greenland.

Answers to Multiple-Choice Questions

1. **D**
2. **B**
3. **C**
4. **A**
5. **B**

Scoring Guides

Struggling readers may provide responses that are less complete than those provided by more advanced readers. You can take this into account when grading students' responses.

Question 6

Complete The response explains why Australia's desert resources need to be conserved and two ways to conserve them. The need for conservation may include that most of these resources are nonrenewable, that they are running out or that they are being used up rapidly. Ways to conserve desert resources may include using less electricity, turning off lights and electrical appliances when they are not in use, using efficient heating or air-conditioning systems, or recycling copper and other materials.

Partial The response includes an explanation for why Australia's desert resources need to be conserved and only one way to do so or two ways to conserve desert resources but no explanation for why.

Unsatisfactory/Incorrect The response includes little or no information related to conserving Australia's desert resources.

Question 7

Complete The response is a complete sentence that tells what the map mostly shows. The response includes information related to Australia's desert resources, such as what they are (coal, natural gas, copper, gold, iron, and opals) and where they are found.

Partial The response is a complete or incomplete sentence that tells what the map partly shows. The response includes some information related to Australia's desert resources, but is not detailed.

Unsatisfactory/Incorrect The response is an incomplete sentence that does not relate to the map. The response does not refer to Australia's desert resources.

Question 8

Complete The response recognizes that iron mining occurs mostly in the western part of Australia and that there is no other resource around these iron mines, that iron is one of the major resources of Australia, or that the iron mines are all quite close together.

Partial The response recognizes one of the above pieces of information about iron mines in Australia.

Unsatisfactory/Incorrect The response does not give any of the above information about the iron mines in Australia.

Answers to Multiple-Choice Questions

1. **D**
2. **B**
3. **C**
4. **A**
5. **B**

Scoring Guides

Struggling readers may provide responses that are less complete than those provided by more advanced readers. You can take this into account when grading students' responses.

Question 6

Complete The response explains why Peru's mountain resources need to be conserved and two ways to conserve them. The need for conservation may include deforestation; the loss of trees; the extinction or endangerment of certain kinds of animals; landslides and soil erosion; that some of these resources are nonrenewable and are running out; or that others are renewable but are being used up faster than they can be replaced. Ways to conserve these resources may include establishing national parks where trees will be protected, recycling copper and other materials, planting new trees, or changing farming methods.

Partial The response includes an explanation for why Peru's mountain resources need to be conserved and only one way to do so or two ways to conserve desert resources but no explanation for why.

Unsatisfactory/Incorrect The response includes little or no information related to conserving Peru's mountain resources.

Question 7

Complete The response is a complete sentence that tells what the map mostly shows. The response includes information related to South America's resources, such as what they are (copper, lead, silver, etc.) and where they are found.

Partial The response is a complete or incomplete sentence that tells what the map partly shows. The response includes some information related to South America's resources, but is not detailed.

Unsatisfactory/Incorrect The response is an incomplete sentence that does not relate to the map. The response does not refer to South America's resources.

Question 8

Complete The response recognizes that copper is found in South America and that it is one of the major resources of South America and that it is found in the west of South America in Peru, Argentina, Brazil, and Bolivia.

Partial The response recognizes one of the above pieces of information about copper in South America.

Unsatisfactory/Incorrect The response does not give any of the above information about copper in South America.

Notes